Strategic
Youth Ministry

by

Eugene C. Roehlkepartain, Margaret R. Hinchey,
I. Shelby Andress, and Jennifer Griffin-Wiesner

Group
Loveland, Colorado

Strategic Youth Ministry

Copyright © 2000 Search Institute

Visit our Web site: **www.grouppublishing.com**

Credits

Editor: Amy Simpson

Creative Development Editor: Jim Kochenburger

Chief Creative Officer: Joani Schultz

Copy Editor: Janis Sampson

Art Director and Designer: Jeff Lane

Computer Graphic Artist: Joyce Douglas

Production Manager: Alexander Jorgensen

Library of Congress Cataloging-in-Publication Data

Strategic youth ministry / by Eugene C. Roehlkepartain ... [et al.].

    p. cm.

   Includes bibliographical references.

   ISBN 0-7644-2189-1

    1. Church work with youth--Lutheran Church--Missouri Synod. 2. Youth--Religious

life. I. Roehlkepartain, Eugene C., 1962-

BV4447 .S7255 2000

292'.23--dc21

                       99-059301

10 9 8 7 6 5 4 3 2 1   09 08 07 06 05 04 03 02 01 00

Printed in the United States of America.

Contents

108599

Acknowledgments

This book has been developed with the support, input, and dedication of many people and organizations to whom we are deeply grateful.

First, major support and guidance for this book were provided through a grant from Lutheran Brotherhood, a member-owned organization of over one million Lutherans joined together for financial security, benevolent outreach, and volunteer service. Special thanks to Beryl Deskin in LB's communications department, who has worked with us as a flexible, encouraging guide, colleague, and friend in this process.

Second, we relied on input and support from many people in the Department of Youth Ministry of The Lutheran Church-Missouri Synod (LCMS), who trusted Search Institute to create a major leadership development track for their Youth Gathering. Thanks especially to LeRoy Wilke and David Weidner, who saw the potential and became allies and partners in our efforts.

In addition to the Youth Ministry Department, this book would not have been possible without the work of Lou Jander in the Adult Ministry Department, who was instrumental in completing the study of LCMS adults and youth that is the basis for this book.

As we formed the vision of how to develop useful resources and training for youth ministry out of the national study of youth and adults, we relied on a Youth Advisory Committee to help shape the focus and content of this book. Members were Jack Giles, Lou Jander, Paul Krentz, Sheryll Mennicke, Kurt Niebuhr, Jim Ollhoff, Cherie Theis, David Weidner, and LeRoy Wilke.

Finally, we thank the team at Group Publishing for seeing the broader potential of this book and for their careful work in publishing this resource. Special thanks to David Thornton, Amy Simpson, and Joani Schultz who have worked with us on this manuscript.

Introduction

"We need more youth activities in our congregation."
"Let's do a servant event this summer."
"Should we do a lock-in again this year?"
"How can we add another youth activity? We're too busy already."

These kinds of questions and statements are common among people involved in youth ministry. There are so many needs, so many ideas, so much that could be done. How do you decide what to do? What are the priorities?

Effective youth ministry helps youth develop a deep and enduring faith. But effective youth ministry is not just a series of programs and projects that keep youth busy, involved, and coming to church. Rather, it results from thoughtful planning in which a congregation becomes intentional about providing opportunities and experiences for youth that can strengthen their faith commitment.

The Research Behind *Strategic Youth Ministry*

Strategic Youth Ministry is based on a major Search Institute study of 2,314 adults and youth in 151 Lutheran Church-Missouri Synod congregations titled *Congregations at Crossroads: A National Study of Adults and Youth in the Lutheran Church-Missouri Synod.* This book not only gives a glimpse of the faith lives of LCMS adults and youth and their experiences in their families and congregations, but also pinpoints qualities in congregations that contribute to growth in faith among youth and adults. Furthermore, it focuses on the study's implications for youth and youth ministry.

At the heart of the study is an exploration of the faith life and experiences of LCMS adults and youth based on the framework of "faith maturity." Developed by Search Institute through several national studies in other denominations, the framework seeks to capture the extent to which individuals embody the priorities, commitments, and perspectives of a dynamic and life-transforming faith. At its core, the Faith Maturity Index measures two basic dimensions of Christian faith:

• the *vertical* dimension, which indicates a life-transforming relationship with a loving God, and

• the *horizontal* dimension, which indicates a consistent devotion to serving others in the world.

Youth and adults in congregations were surveyed regarding their personal commitments, actions, and beliefs. Based on their responses, people were scored on the two dimensions. Ideally, people would score high on both these dimensions, indicating what we call an "integrated" faith.

Congregations have a great deal of influence on the shape of faith, beliefs, and actions of youth and adults. This study identified thirty-four qualities of congregational life that correlate with young people having an integrated faith, growing in faith, and being loyal to their congregation and denomination. As young people experience more of these qualities, they are more likely to experience a life-transforming faith. Yet the average LCMS youth experiences only 12.1 of these faith-nurturing qualities.

These thirty-four qualities are certainly not the only things that are important in youth ministry, but they do provide an important place to start thinking about what it means to be a faith-nurturing congregation for youth. By seeking to build these qualities, congregations have great potential for renewing and enhancing members' faith and their commitments to live that faith and share that faith with others through acts of evangelism, outreach, and service.

Practical Ideas

Strategic Youth Ministry focuses on the practical ways you can strengthen your youth ministry in thirty-four areas that were found to be key in nurturing faith in adolescents. Here's what you'll find:

The first section introduces the dimensions of faith maturity and helps you reflect on your priorities in youth ministry. It also introduces the qualities identified through research that are important for nurturing a mature faith in youth.

Each remaining chapter focuses on a broad area of

congregational life that we found to be important in nurturing faith. These range from an engaging climate to effective Christian education to inspiring worship. You'll find brief background information on each of these areas, plus a work sheet to help you and your planning team evaluate your congregation in each area.

Within each of these major areas, we have identified keys to effective youth ministry. For each key you'll find creative, practical ideas to use in your congregation. These ideas can be used as they are or as triggers for additional brainstorming about what would work best in your setting. In addition, you'll be pointed toward other resources if you need to focus on a specific area, recognizing that this book introduces topics and themes, but does not explore them in depth. (See Resource Publishers on page 123.)

Within each section you'll find at least one work sheet to help teenagers read Scripture, pray, discuss, and write about their faith in the context of church life. These tools will help young people understand the keys discussed and apply these concepts to their church experience. They'll also give teenagers opportunities to look for and incorporate those elements in their lives. These pieces will then help teenagers and church leaders work together to act on the students' feedback.

Section 10 offers four sessions (each about one hour long) to help your congregation reflect on the implications of the study's findings and framework for your youth ministry. While it presents some information from the national study, it also focuses on helping your congregation explore its own faith life and on ways to strengthen youth ministry. By using these four sessions, you'll

■ help participants reflect on the dimensions of faith and their implications for your congregation's youth ministry (session 1),

■ examine your congregation in light of thirty-four qualities of congregations that nurture young people's faith (session 2),

■ begin envisioning and setting priorities for how your congregation hopes to shape its youth ministry (session 3), and

■ identify ways to begin working toward your priorities and building support for your vision (session 4).

Using *Strategic Youth Ministry* for Planning

Strategic Youth Ministry has been written so that you can use it many different ways. Most people won't read through it cover to cover. Rather, you can dip into it to get help in specific areas of interest.

It also includes many tools that can be useful for getting the big picture and planning your congregation's youth ministry. Here's a simple way to use the book for planning:

1. Get a cross section of youth and adults together for a planning session. (Include adults who are not active youth program volunteers.) Introduce some of the key ideas in this book.

2. Focus attention on the introductory page and work sheet for each of the eight categories. Perhaps assign each of these areas to a small group to present to everyone else. Ask each group to introduce its quality, why it thinks the quality is important, and how well it believes the congregation is doing in that particular area. Have groups use the work sheets as tools to assess how the congregation is doing. Have them complete the exercises for teenagers and discuss them.

3. After all the small groups have made their presentations, have the whole group identify the top strengths in the congregation and the areas of greatest need and concern. Use these ideas and the four sessions to focus energy in the youth ministry. Use the specific ideas for the individual qualities to develop ideas and plans.

As you develop plans, don't feel that you have to do everything—or that everything is even appropriate for your congregation. Use this book (and others like it) to spark your own thinking and creativity. Then use the shared knowledge, commitments, and sense of calling of your congregation to shape the kind of ministry that will most impact the lives of young people in your congregation and community.

Notes on This Book

Focus on Youth

Strategic Youth Ministry focuses on how youth ministry affects young people's faith. In doing so, it broadens and shapes the findings from research to application by helping you apply the findings directly to your youth ministry. For example, while the study zeroed in on the pastor's leadership style, this book expands this quality to suggest that all the leadership in youth ministry—including clergy—is more effective when its style is open and affirming.

In preparing this resource, we recognize that there are many ways to strengthen youth ministry to nurture faith in young people. Other factors may be important. Other ideas may work better for you. However, we hope that these insights and ideas will help to generate a renewed focus and new energy that strengthen your congregation's ability to serve youth and cultivate in them a lifelong, life-changing faith.

Focusing

A Search Institute study of religious youth workers from many different denominations found that only about two out of five said their congregation has a mission statement for youth work. This finding may say something about why youth ministry has such a high burnout rate: Volunteers invest a lot of time, energy, and commitment in youth ministry without having a clear sense of what the congregation hopes to accomplish through that ministry.

The four sessions offered in this book provide an opportunity for your congregation to reflect on what it hopes to offer that will shape the faith and lives of young people. This process can renew energy and enthusiasm for those involved and can also help to ensure that your congregation's efforts are truly having a life-changing impact on young people.

Section 1:

Nurturing Faith–
A Focus for Youth Ministry

Nurturing Faith– A Focus for Youth Ministry

What is the goal of your youth ministry? While some youth workers have a clear sense of mission, many have trouble answering this key question. Some programs are offered because they've always been. Others happen because that's what the denomination recommends. And still others occur simply because someone wanted to do them.

However, when you reflect on the underlying, core reasons for youth ministry, two basic purposes (or variations of them) will likely surface:

• to nurture in young people a faith that expresses itself in a strong commitment to Jesus Christ, and in compassion, service, and outreach to others in the world; and

• to help guide youth to make positive, healthy choices in life.

Of course, each congregation will shape those goals a little differently and give each one different emphasis. Furthermore, some will argue that the two goals are really the same, since nurturing a lifelong faith will lead young people to make positive choices.

However, naming these two interlocking purposes provides a foundation upon which to build an effective youth ministry. After all, just as it's impossible to construct a useful building without knowing why you're building it, it's impossible to design an effective, top-quality youth program without knowing its purpose.

Because of the focus of the research on LCMS youth and adults, this book emphasizes the goal of nurturing faith. Other Search Institute work focuses on how congregations nurture healthy development.[1] In addition, many of the same factors that nurture faith are also important for young people's healthy development.

What Is Faith Maturity?

If congregations are committed to helping young people grow in their faith and live their faith in the world, then it's important to think first about what we mean by faith and faith maturity.

No one knows exactly how God is working to transform and shape people's lives. So any effort to name specific characteristics of a person with a mature faith is risky. At the same time, Christians believe faith shapes what they do—what they believe, how they live their lives in the world.

Two Dimensions of Faith

To begin the conversation, Search Institute has worked with theologians, pastors, denominational leaders, and others to construct a framework called faith maturity. It doesn't measure whether people have faith, but indicates how they express their faith. To discern faith maturity, faith is measured in two dimensions:

• The *vertical* dimension indicates a life-transforming relationship with God. People express this dimension of faith by worshipping God, praying, and seeking opportunities for spiritual growth.

• The *horizontal* dimension indicates a consistent devotion to serving others in the world. People express this dimension of faith by helping people in need, getting involved in social issues, and sharing their faith with others.

In an ideal world, most people would express both of these dimensions of faith. However, when we examine LCMS youth nationally, we find that 25 percent express a faith that is strong in both dimensions—an "integrated" faith. Indeed, most young people's faith expression is low in both dimensions—an "undeveloped" faith.

Nine Marks of Faith

Another way to think about faith maturity is to examine "nine marks" of faith. These are nine attitudes and behaviors of people who express a well-rounded, mature faith. The following nine marks include many of the dimensions of Christian discipleship:

• trusting in God's saving grace and believing firmly in the humanity and divinity of Jesus;

• experiencing a sense of personal well-being, security, and peace (the fruits of faith);

• integrating faith and life—seeing work, family, and social relationships as part of one's religious life;

• celebrating the good news of God's work in individual lives; [2]

• seeking spiritual growth through study, reflection, prayer, and discussion with others;

• seeking to be part of a community of believers in which people give witness to their faith and support and nurture one another;

• holding life-affirming values, including a commitment to racial and gender equity, affirmation of cultural and religious diversity, and a personal sense of responsibility for the welfare of others;

• advocating social change to improve human welfare; and

• serving humanity, consistently and passionately, through acts of love and compassion.

Work Sheet 1
Reflecting on Your Faith

Use this work sheet to reflect on your own faith experiences through the framework of Search Institute's nine marks of faith maturity. Invite youth and parents to use the work sheet as well, then talk about your experiences, priorities, and struggles.

How Much Do You...	A Little	Some	A Lot
1. Experience God's presence, grace, and unconditional love guiding you in your life?	❏	❏	❏
2. Experience a sense of peace, freedom, security, purpose, and self-acceptance that grows out of your faith?	❏	❏	❏
3. Rely on your faith to guide your daily decisions, your moral values, and your views on social and political issues?	❏	❏	❏
4. Share your faith with others and celebrate Christ's transforming work in people's lives?	❏	❏	❏
5. Seek opportunities for ongoing spiritual growth through prayer, Bible study, and other spiritual disciplines?	❏	❏	❏
6. Spend time in a Christian community where you nurture the faith of others, share your faith story, and experience God's presence?	❏	❏	❏
7. Take care of your health, celebrate diversity, and affirm the dignity of all people?	❏	❏	❏
8. Believe your faith demands global and political concern and involvement to improve the welfare of other people?	❏	❏	❏
9. Live out your faith by spending time serving people in need, promoting justice, protecting the environment, and promoting peace?	❏	❏	❏

STRATEGIC YOUTH MINISTRY

• What memories did completing this checklist evoke in you?

• What surprises or insights about yourself did you discover as you completed the checklist?

• In what way does this framework challenge you to grow in your faith?

Published in *Strategic Youth Ministry* by Group Publishing, Inc., P.O. Box 481, Loveland, CO 80539.

Work Sheet 2

Nurturing Faith: Youth Ministry Emphases

Each congregation emphasizes different things in its youth ministry. To evaluate your priorities, first decide how important each mark of faith should be in your youth ministry. Then reflect on how well you do in this area. When you see gaps between importance and achievement, reflect on ways you could celebrate strengths and improve in areas with the greatest gaps.

Mark of Faith	How Important? (1 = low; 5 = high)	How Well Do You Do? (1 = not well; 5 = very well)	Ideas for Celebrating and Improving the Emphasis on Each Mark of Faith
1. Trusting and believing			
2. Experiencing the fruits of faith			
3. Integrating faith and life			
4. Celebrating the good news			
5. Seeking spiritual growth			
6. Nurturing faith in community			
7. Holding life-affirming values			
8. Advocating social change			
9. Acting and serving			

Published in *Strategic Youth Ministry* by Group Publishing, Inc., P.O. Box 481, Loveland, CO 80539.

Learning Together
Youth Handout
Reflecting on Your Faith

Some theologians, pastors, and educators worked together to identify nine areas, or marks, of faith that are important to cultivate. At their core, these nine marks fit into two dimensions of faith. First is a relationship to a loving God (also called the vertical dimension of faith). Second is a commitment to serving others and the world (also called the horizontal dimension of faith). The challenge for Christians is to build strengths in both dimensions for a mature faith.

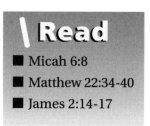

▌Read

■ Micah 6:8

■ Matthew 22:34-40

■ James 2:14-17

- -

²Reflect

▌ Which of the nine marks of faith do you see as a strength for you (see the "React" section below)? Which ones pose the greatest challenges?

▌ How do the passages from Micah and Matthew (see above) challenge you? Is it more in the area of horizontal faith (serving others, doing justice) or vertical faith (loving God, walking humbly with God)?

▌ Which of the nine dimensions of faith are most emphasized in your congregation? Which ones aren't dealt with much? Why do you think that is?

³React

Use this checklist—which is loosely based on these nine areas—to think about the things you emphasize in your own faith…and where you may need to grow. Then talk with your group members about what you discovered.

How Much Do You...	A Little	Some	A Lot
1. Experience God's presence, grace, and unconditional love guiding you in your life?	❏	❏	❏
2. Experience a sense of peace, freedom, security, purpose, and self-acceptance that grows out of your faith?	❏	❏	❏
3. Rely on your faith to guide your daily decisions, your moral values, and your views on social and political issues?	❏	❏	❏
4. Share your faith with others and celebrate Christ's transforming work in people's lives?	❏	❏	❏
5. Seek opportunities for ongoing spiritual growth through prayer, Bible study, and other spiritual disciplines?	❏	❏	❏
6. Spend time in Christian community where you nurture the faith of others, share your faith story, and experience God's presence?	❏	❏	❏
7. Take care of your health, celebrate diversity, and affirm the dignity of all people?	❏	❏	❏
8. Believe your faith demands global and political concern and involvement to improve the welfare of other people?	❏	❏	❏
9. Live out your faith by spending time serving people in need, promoting justice, protecting the environment, and promoting peace?	❏	❏	❏

⁴Respond

The nine marks of faith are certainly not the final word on the dimensions of faith. Talk to your parent(s), pastor, youth leader, other adults, and peers about what they see as core elements of the faith. Use the opportunity to get to know them better—and to better understand and articulate your own faith.

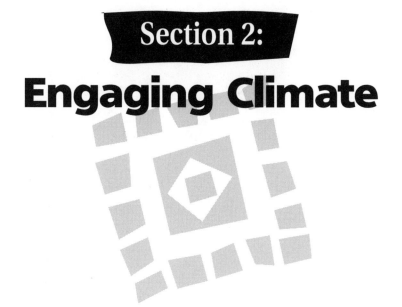

Section 2:

Engaging Climate

Engaging Climate

One reason people talk about the weather so much is that it makes a big difference in our daily lives. It can affect how we feel, what we do, how we interact with others. A drizzly day can dampen spirits; a sunny day can bring energy and joy.

The climate of congregations has a similar impact on young people's faith. When a congregation is warm, intellectually challenging, open to change, and free of conflict, youth are more likely to thrive. When it's heavy, suspicious, boring, and lifeless, it drains their interest and involvement—much like a hot, muggy day.

Many youth do not experience a climate in their church that is warm, challenging, exciting, and free of conflict. However, when present, these qualities provide the kind of atmosphere where young people's faith and commitment are more likely to grow.

Work Sheet 3
Evaluating Your Congregation's Climate

Use this work sheet to think about the climate of your congregation. First, rate your congregation on each of the items in the second column. Then list in the third column things you do already to strengthen each quality. Finally, jot down other things you could do to improve your congregation's climate.

Qualities	Rating Your Congregation Needs Work = * OK = ** Great = ***	What We Do Now	What We Could Do Better
Warm climate	___ The congregation feels warm to youth. ___ The congregation accepts youth who are different. ___ The congregation is friendly to youth. ___ People care about youth in the congregation. ___ People in the congregation take time to get to know youth.		
Thinking climate	___ Young people learn a lot from the congregation. ___ The congregation expects youth to learn and think. ___ The congregation is open to new ideas. ___ The congregation challenges young people's thinking. ___ The congregation encourages youth to ask questions.		
Lack of conflict	___ There is not a lot of conflict and disagreement in the congregation. ___ There is not a lot of conflict and disagreement in the youth program.		
Excitement	___ Youth are excited about the congregation and its youth ministry.		
Intergenerational interaction	___ Youth and adults in the congregation spend time together.		

Create a Warm, Welcoming, and Friendly Climate

What it is

Youth are much more likely to grow in their faith when their congregation is a warm, friendly, caring, inviting community of faith. What does a "warm" youth program look like? It's a place where...

■ youth and adults are friendly to youth.

■ visitors and newcomers (including youth) feel welcomed.

■ all young people feel welcomed and included in the group.

■ people in the congregation and youth program know young people by their names.

Talk with youth

■ What are ways that you experience the congregation and its young people to be "warm"? How do they come across as "cold"?

■ How would you rate our congregation in the various dimensions of a warm climate? What areas are strengths? What are the concerns?

■ How do young people treat newcomers? Do newcomers experience a warm and friendly environment?

During a youth meeting, give each person a photocopy of the "Learning Together: Warming Up Relationships" handout on page 21. Instruct youth to form groups of three to five, and have group members work through their handouts together.

Ideas to try

■ Make group-building activities a regular part of your youth and education programs.

■ Use youth greeters in pairs (preferably male and female together) to meet younger kids when they arrive for congregational activities.

■ Give youth greeters a supply of coupons for visitors to receive a free doughnut at a youth-sponsored doughnut table on Sunday mornings.

■ Evaluate how you treat youth in your congregation. Do you pay more attention to your favorites? How can you reach out to those who may be new or less involved?

■ Involve youth as teen sponsors in new member programs for the whole congregation.

Resources to use

Patrick Kiefert, **Welcoming the Stranger** *(Augsburg Fortress Publishers).*

Thomas G. Kirkpatrick, **Small Groups in the Church: A Handbook for Creating Community** *(Alban Institute).*

Denny Rydberg, **Youth Group Trust Builders** *(Group Publishing).*

Learning Together
Youth Handout

Warming Up Relationships

If someone new visited your youth group, would he or she describe the group as warm, friendly, and welcoming? And—just as important—do people who come every week feel like they are welcomed and valued? Unless people are accepted and welcomed into a congregation or youth group, they are unlikely to become active or to benefit as much from their involvement.

Read
- Luke 7:36-50
- Acts 9:26-27
- 1 Corinthians 11:17-34

---

2 Reflect

What do these Bible passages suggest about the ways your congregation and youth program welcome others?

How do you act when a newcomer visits your congregation? What could you to do make her or him feel more welcome?

How can you help make your congregation a warm place for the regular attenders, some of whom may feel lonely?

If you don't feel accepted in your congregation and youth program, who can you talk to about it? What might you do to help others open up to you?

3 React

First impressions often have a lasting impact. Do you remember the first time you went to a new school? Who did you see? What did you notice about the building? Did anyone talk to you? What did you like about it? What did you dislike? Who made you feel the most welcome? Write a story about your first day at a new school, a new church, or another new place. After the story is written, trade stories with your group members, and read what they wrote.

Now brainstorm with your group about what it would be like for a new person joining your congregation. Write down three things you can do to help make your congregation a more welcoming place for newcomers.

1: _____

_____

2: _____

_____

3: _____

_____

4 Respond

One Sunday, visit another congregation in your community (or in another community when you're out of town) where you don't know anyone. Pay attention to the ways people make you feel comfortable...and uncomfortable. Use the experience to think about and work to improve the way your own congregation expresses warmth and friendliness.

Key 2

Cultivate a Climate That Challenges Young People's Thinking

What it is

When youth come to church, do they put their brains in neutral? If so, they're less likely to grow in their faith. Congregations are most likely to stimulate young people's growth (and keep them interested) if the climate encourages thinking and questioning. Being open to tough questions—about anything—and giving young people safe places to ask those questions are keys to creating a climate in which their faith can thrive. A thinking climate is probably in place when…

■ young people say they learn a lot in their congregation.

■ most members want to be challenged to think about religious questions and issues.

■ young people are encouraged to ask questions and are expected to learn and think.

■ the congregation is open to new ideas.

Resources to use

Mike Yaconelli and Scott Koenigsaecker, **Get 'em Talking!** *(Youth Specialties).*

Group's Best Discussion Launchers for Youth Ministry *(Group Publishing).*

Talk with youth

■ In which church activities is your thinking most challenged? least challenged?

■ What questions do you have that you wish you could talk about in church?

■ How do you think new ideas are received in this congregation?

During a youth meeting, give each person a photocopy of the "Learning Together: Think Fast!" handout on page 23. Instruct youth to work through their handouts individually, then to form pairs for the "Respond" section.

Ideas to try

■ Provide midweek youth forums that include outside speakers or facilitators on topics that interest youth and adults.

■ Survey youth to find out topics they have questions about. Sponsor youth programs that feature discussions of those questions.

■ Include one or two questions in the weekly newsletter or worship bulletin that lead youth and families into discussions on the sermon or the Scripture reading of the day.

■ Devote a section of the congregation's library to books and periodicals that interest youth.

Learning Together
Youth Handout

Think Fast!

When Jesus told parables, he often left people scratching their heads. "What did he mean by that?" "I don't understand." Jesus rarely explained things too much. Rather, he challenged people to think for themselves. When they do, the answers are much more likely to stick with them.

The same is true with our faith and in our church life. If we're never challenged to think for ourselves, we're likely to get lazy about what we believe and think. When people cut off our questions and try to spoon-feed us with answers, we can get bored. When we experience a climate that challenges us to think for ourselves, our understanding of our faith is stimulated and grows.

1 Read
- Matthew 13:24-30
- Luke 16:19-31

2 Reflect

■ Why do you think Jesus didn't tell people the meaning of these parables? How might the original hearers of these parables have responded? In what ways do these parables challenge you to think?

■ What has been the most thought-provoking experience for you in your congregation in the past year? What made it challenge your thinking?

■ Who are the people in your congregation you can go to when you have questions or want to talk about things?

3 React

Issue	Ways My Church Challenges Me to Think About This Issue
Bible	
Dating	
Environment	
Family	
Friends	
God, Jesus, and the Holy Spirit	
Myself	
School	
Violence	
Others	

4 Respond

Find a partner and talk to that person about an issue you feel is important or that you struggle with. Use the work sheet in the "React" section to come up with ideas. Together, come up with at least one idea for addressing the issue.

_____

_____

_____

Minimize Conflict...and Deal With It Constructively When It Arises

What it is

Conflict, according to the dictionary, is "a prolonged battle, struggle, clash" or "controversy, disagreement, opposition." Those are not the kinds of words we like applying to congregations. When people's fists are clenched in conflict, they can't open their hands to give or receive.

Of course, some conflict is inevitable, since people bring different perspectives, priorities, and needs to their congregation and the youth program. When that occurs, the challenge is to find ways to resolve the conflict compassionately and with integrity so that healing and renewed commitment grow out of the disagreements.

Talk with youth

■ How much conflict do you sense is present in this congregation? in the youth program? What areas of congregational life seem to experience the most conflict?

■ When conflicts arise in the youth ministry program, how do we typically respond? Is our response healthy, or are there other approaches that might be more healing?

During a youth meeting, give each person a photocopy of the "Learning Together: Good Conflict/Bad Conflict" handout on page 25. Tell youth they'll need to find partners for the "React" section.

Ideas to try

■ Ask the pastor, Christian education director, and other congregational leaders to visit with the youth on their turf once each quarter to hear their ideas, insights, and concerns about the church.

■ Make an extra effort to ensure that accurate and adequate information is provided to all parents and youth regarding the congregation's youth ministry activities and philosophy.

■ Regularly seek honest feedback from youth, parents, and other members about the youth program. Provide opportunities for people to give feedback anonymously (for example, by using a suggestion box).

■ Train both youth and adults in conflict-resolution skills, and encourage them to use those skills in youth and adult programs.

Resources to use

Charles H. Cosgrove and Dennis D. Hatfield, **Church Conflict: The Hidden Systems Behind the Fights** *(Abingdon Press).*

Lloyd Edwards, **How We Belong, Fight, and Pray** *(Alban Institute).*

Kenneth C. Haugk, **Antagonists in the Church: How to Identify and Deal With Destructive Conflict** *(Augsburg Fortress Publishers).*

Learning Together

Good Conflict/Bad Conflict

Conflict can be very harmful and destructive, leaving people wounded and angry. But it can also be a positive sign of growth, energy, and change. How do you know the difference?

There's no quick formula. But one question to ask is, What's at stake? If underlying the conflict is a battle of egos and personalities, the conflict is probably more harmful than helpful. But if the conflict is challenging those involved to struggle with priorities and their sense of purpose and direction, that conflict may be very positive—even if it's not very comfortable.

Congregations that help people grow in faith know how to deal well with conflict. Knowing the difference between good and bad conflict is a great place to begin.

Read

■ Jonah 3:1–4:11

■ Luke 9:46-50

■ 1 Corinthians 1:10-17

2 Reflect

▪ The Bible passages above all tell stories of people in conflict. What insights do these stories give regarding the difference between good and bad conflict?

▪ Think about a time when you have experienced conflict in your congregation. What was at stake in the conflict? What positive things did the congregation do to handle the conflict?

▪ What are some ways you can minimize harmful conflict with others in your congregation while working constructively through negative conflict?

3 React

The most effective way for people to achieve their goals is to work cooperatively. When one person tries to keep others down, everyone loses. In addition, when one person lets everyone else do the work (or make the decisions), no one gets what he or she really wants. Try the following activity to find out more about working together toward a common goal.

The object of this activity is to get into a standing position without using your arms or hands to help you. Unfortunately, both you and your partner want the same thing, but *not* for each other.

1. Find a partner to help you with this exercise.

2. Sit on the floor with your partner, back to back. Lock arms with your partner or cross them in front of you.

3. Without either you or your partner putting hands on the floor, try to stand up without letting your partner stand up.

4. Now, let your partner try to stand up and pick you up, too. Don't help!

5. Finally, work cooperatively with your partner to see if you can both stand up.

After you have completed the exercise, discuss these questions with your partner:

• Which time was it the easiest for you to stand up? Why?

• Which time was it the easiest for your partner to stand up? Why?

• What happened when you were very aggressive and tried to keep your partner down?

• What happened when you were very passive and let your partner do all the work?

4 Respond

Ask several adults in the congregation to tell you their perspective on a current conflict within your congregation. (It doesn't have to be a major conflict.) Try to uncover the underlying issues in the conflict. Decide whether you think the conflict is dealing with an important difference in priorities or whether it's more about personality differences or miscommunication.

Generate Excitement for the Congregation's Youth Ministry

What it is

In some ways, excitement is the icing on the cake in youth ministry. True, you can have good programs without excitement. Young people can be nourished and grow. But like frosting, excitement can make the difference between an "OK" retreat and a "Fantastic!" retreat. It can make the difference between youth wandering in and out of meetings (mentally, if not physically) and being interested and engaged.

However, too much excitement without substance is like eating a lot of frosting without cake—very unsatisfying. The goal is to offer a balance of relationships, opportunities, and insights that will excite youth and make them eager to come back for more.

Talk with youth

■ What are the things that most excite you about our congregation and youth ministry program?

■ What could we do to make our youth ministry program more exciting for you?

Ideas to try

■ Take time to publicly celebrate completed programs, successful events, and personal accomplishments of both youth and adults.

■ Take time to publicize all youth activities—not just to get young people to participate, but also to build energy and excitement among other members of the congregation.

■ Encourage youth to participate in an annual ministry fair that shares information about the programs and opportunities for service in the congregation.

Resources to use

The Church Art Works, **Youth Workers' Promo Kit** *(Youth Specialties).*

Terry Dittmer, **Youth Ministry Sketchbook: 130 Practical Ideas for Ministry** *(Concordia Publishing House).*

Rand Kruback, **Outrageous Clip Art for Youth Ministry** *(Group Publishing).*

Provide Opportunities for Youth and Adults to Spend Quality Time Together

What it is

We live in a society that is highly age-segregated. Senior citizens spend time with senior citizens. Youth spend time with youth. Young adults spend time with young adults. While everyone enjoys building relationships with people who are in the same stage in life, there's also a richness in relationships across generations. Young people have much to learn from the wisdom and deep faith of older church members. Older members can be reinvigorated by and learn from their relationships with youth.

Talk with youth

■ How many adults do you know well in the congregation? How do these relationships make you feel about the congregation?

■ Who is one of your favorite adults in the congregation? Why?

■ What kinds of activities would you like to do together with adults in the congregation?

During a youth meeting, give each person a photocopy of the "Learning Together: Young, Old, In Between" handout on page 28. Instruct youth to form pairs and work through their handouts together.

Ideas to try

■ Use adults as mentors to develop significant relationships with youth from confirmation through high school.

■ Involve youth and adults together in projects such as serving midweek meals, congregational clean-up days, and other activities.

■ Offer intergenerational activity nights quarterly. Ask youth and older adults to help plan them together.

Resources to use

Mark DeVries and Nan Russell, **Bridges: 15 Sessions to Connect Youth and Adults** *(InterVarsity Press).*

Jolene L. Roehlkepartain, **Creating Intergenerational Community: 75 Ideas for Building Relationships Between Young People and Adults** *(Search Institute).*

James W. White, **Intergenerational Religious Education** *(Religious Education Press).*

No More Us & Them: 100 Ways to Bring Your Youth & Church Together *(Group Publishing).*

Learning Together
Youth Handout

Young, Old, In Between

It's easy to spend all our time with people our own age. After all, we share a lot of interests with them, we go to a lot of the same places they do, and we tend to see things in similar ways. But building relationships with other generations—younger children and adults of all ages—can enrich our lives and our faith in important ways.

Read

- Numbers 11:16-17
- Proverbs 16:31; 20:29
- Matthew 18:10
- 1 Timothy 4:12-14

- -

2 Reflect

According to these Bible passages, there is value in knowing people of all different ages. How many of the important relationships in your life are with people who are younger than you? How many are with adults close to your parents' age? How many are with older adults or senior citizens?

What do you most value about relationships with people of different ages? What makes them difficult or awkward?

3 React

Pick one person who isn't your age and whom you feel close to, and write about that person. Describe that person's appearance and behavior. Why do you like her or him? Describe your relationship. How did you meet and what kinds of things do you do together?

Now share what you wrote with your partner. Discuss ways you can show your appreciation to the person you wrote about.

4 Respond

Identify a senior, longtime member of your congregation who you would like to get to know better. (If you don't know any seniors, ask your youth leader or a parent for some suggestions.) Ask if he or she would be willing to spend time talking with you about memories of the congregation over the years. Use the questions below to get started.

- How long have you been a member of our congregation?
- What was the congregation like when you first joined?
- What are some of the major events you remember happening in the congregation?
- How many pastors have been here since you joined?
- What do you like most about our congregation?
- What about our congregation concerns you?
- Are you involved in any congregational activities?
- How many young people in the congregation do you know well?
- What's a funny story you remember about something that happened in our congregation?

STRATEGIC YOUTH MINISTRY

Section 3:

Caring Community

Caring Community

In addition to creating a nurturing climate, faith-nurturing congregations also emphasize creating a community in which young people feel cared for and through which they can express care and concern for people in the community.

The youth ministry often forms a caring community for youth. Community-building exercises are common at youth meetings, camps, and retreats. However, most of the focus is on caring peer relationships. Often youth are ignored—or even avoided—by many other members of the congregation. Like the rest of society, too many congregations are age-segregated, with each generation pretty much sticking to itself.

While peer relationships are important, it's important for young people to nurture caring relationships with members in the larger community of faith. These relationships not only give young people someone to talk with who is caring and principled, but they also can help young people see mature faith "in action" in the lives of people of the faith.

The challenge, then, is not only to help youth know that their youth group is a caring community, but that the whole faith community is also a caring and loving place for them. When that happens, they are much more likely to turn to the church when they are struggling or celebrating.

Work Sheet 4

Evaluating Your Congregation's Sense of Caring Community

Use this work sheet to reflect on the many dimensions of caring in your congregation. First, rate your congregation on each of the items in the second column. Then, list in the third column things you already do to strengthen each quality. Finally, jot down other things you could do to make your congregation a more caring community for youth.

Qualities	Rating Your Congregation Needs Work = * OK = ** Great = ***	What We Do Now	What We Could Do Better
Meeting personal needs	___ People are good at showing love and concern for each other. ___ The congregation provides members with love, support, and friendship. ___ The congregation helps members find meaning and purpose in their lives. ___ The congregation gives members the strength they need to face the stresses of everyday life. ___ The congregation does a good job of supporting members in times of personal crisis.		
Expressing care	___ People feel that others in the congregation care about them.		
Building relationships	___ People take time to get to know each other.		
Caring for the community	___ The congregation is active in helping people in the community. ___ The congregation involves many people in helping others. ___ The congregation reaches out to the poor and hungry in the community.		
Caring from adults	___ Young people feel the care and support of adults in the congregation.		

Focus on Meeting Youth's Personal Needs

What it is

Young people have important needs that they bring with them to their faith community. Some need special support and care that they receive nowhere else in their lives. Some need to be able to ask tough questions. Some need opportunities to use their gifts and talents to serve a greater good. Some need comfort in the midst of a crisis or loss.

Effective congregations take young people where they are, seek to meet their needs, and draw them into the community of faith. However, that cannot happen until young people are listened to and concerted effort is made to understand their lives and world. It's not always easy or comfortable. But it can make an incredible difference in the impact your congregation has on youth.

Talk with youth

■ If you were to list five things that today's young people need from their congregations, what would you list?

■ In your experience, what are areas where this congregation has most effectively addressed the needs of youth? In what areas have we not done as well?

■ What are some ways our congregation could more effectively address the needs of you and your friends?

Ideas to try

■ Take a survey of youth in your congregation (and ask them to survey their friends). Ask about their experiences, interests, and needs. Use the findings to help shape your youth program.

■ Use youth "deacons" to provide special care to youth and their families.

■ Start a youth prayer chain that youth can access when they or their friends have particular needs. (In addition, be sure to include youth concerns in the whole congregation's prayer concerns.)

■ Include a prayer time in all youth meetings, Sunday school classes, youth choir rehearsals, and other events. Take prayer requests from the group.

Resources to use

Rick Bundschuh and E.G. Von Trutzchler, **Incredible Questionnaires for Youth Ministry** (Youth Specialties).

Peter L. Benson and Eugene C. Roehlkepartain, **Youth in Protestant Churches** (Search Institute).

Merton P. Strommen, **Self-Portrait: A Survey for Young People About Matters of Faith** (Concordia Publishing House).

Dr. G. Keith Olson, **Counseling Teenagers** (Group Publishing).

Scott Larson and David Van Patten, **Quick Connect** (Group Publishing).

Create a Community in Which Youth Experience Support and Care

What it is

Reflect back on your own experiences growing up in the church. What are some things that stand out for you as positive experiences? If you're like most adults, the first thing you remember is a person—or group of people—who really showed they cared about you. Perhaps it was a Sunday school teacher, the youth group, a youth leader.

Providing that kind of support and care tills the soil for effective youth ministry. If young people don't feel cared for in their congregation, it's unlikely that any of the other things you do to help them grow in their faith will take root and flourish.

Resources to use

Kenneth Haugk, **Christian Caregiving: A Way of Life** *(Augsburg Fortress Publishers).*

Walt Marcum, **Sharing Groups in Youth Ministry** *(Abingdon Press).*

Jolene L. Roehlkepartain, **150 Ways to Show Kids You Care** *(Search Institute).*

Michael D. Warden, **Small-Group Body Builders** *(Group Publishing).*

Talk with youth

■ Tell about a time you or your family experienced care and support in the congregation. How did that experience affect you?

■ What happens in the congregation that interferes with you experiencing care and support from other youth? from adults?

■ What kinds of relationships do you have with adults in the congregation who are not directly connected to youth ministry? How could you strengthen these relationships?

Ideas to try

■ Keep a supply of postcards on hand to mail to youth who are ill, frequently absent, or troubled. Similarly remember those who have something to celebrate, such as a graduation, a birthday, or achieving a spot on the honor roll.

■ Train youth to be peer ministers who provide support and care for other youth.

■ As a congregation, commit to ensuring that each young person is known (and greeted every week) by at least five adults in the congregation. If the youth don't attend, have someone call them to check in and find out how things are going.

■ In corporate worship, celebrate significant life passages for youth, including beginning of confirmation instruction, first Communion, confirmation, and graduation.

SECTION 3: CARING COMMUNITY

Provide Opportunities for Youth to Build Relationships With Each Other

What it is

One key to creating a caring community for youth is providing opportunities for them to get to know each other. In the past, we may have been able to assume that those relationships can form elsewhere: in school, in the neighborhood, or elsewhere in the community. Today, however, youth in a congregation may attend many different schools and live in different parts of the city. As a result, congregational activities may be the only place young people see each other.

Nurturing these relationships is not simply a nice idea. If young people have quality relationships with one another within their congregation, they are more likely to be positive influences on each other. Furthermore, they are more likely to stay actively involved in the congregation if they have strong, caring relationships with their friends from church.

Talk with youth

■ How would you describe your relationships with other youth in the congregation? What would strengthen those relationships?

■ What kinds of activities most help you build relationships with other youth?

■ Do you feel there are enough opportunities to get to know other youth in the congregation? If not, what other opportunities could be created?

Ideas to try

■ Begin each youth activity by "touching base" to give young people a chance to share what's happening in their lives.

■ If your group is large, encourage all youth to wear name tags whenever you get together.

■ Take time to introduce each other each time you get together. Use creative questions to get to know each other better. For example, have people give their names and tell what they normally do on Thursdays.

■ Have youth tell about themselves as part of lessons and group discussions.

Resources to use

Wayne Rice, **Up Close and Personal** *(Youth Specialties).*

Jolene L. Roehlkepartain, **Building Assets Together: 135 Group Activities for Helping Youth Succeed** *(Search Institute).*

Denny Rydberg, **Building Community in Youth Groups** *(Group Publishing).*

Denny Rydberg, **Youth Group Trust Builders** *(Group Publishing).*

Connect Youth With Adults in the Congregation

What it is

In most congregations, youth spend very little time with people who are not their age. They rarely interact with younger children, and the only adults they spend time with are the ones who volunteer in the youth program or Christian education program. And while older members of congregations often have the deepest, most mature faith, young people rarely spend time with them.

A key to nurturing young people's faith is to connect them with the larger community of faith, the whole congregation. By building relationships with many adults in the congregation, youth not only form positive, caring relationships, but they also come to know and respect "sages of the faith" who can be mentors and guides along their faith journey.

Talk with youth

■ Who are some of the adults in the congregation who you respect a great deal? What is it about them that attracts you?

■ What are some things you wish you could do with adults in the congregation? What could young people do to get those things to happen?

During a youth meeting, give each person a photocopy of the "Learning Together: Getting to Know You" handout on page 36. Instruct youth to work through their handouts individually or in pairs.

Ideas to try

■ Assign adult prayer partners to pray for members of the confirmation class through the years of their instruction.

■ Match adult mentors with youth between confirmation and graduating from high school. Suggest actions and activities that adults and youth can do together.

■ Continuously encourage adults in the congregation to reach out to children and youth by saying hi to them, sending them birthday cards, helping out with Christian education or youth ministry activities, attending their school events, and otherwise showing interest and care.

■ Keep a list of adults who can be referrals for youth in times of stress, such as loss of a friend or parent, a move to another city, or family conflict.

Resources to use

Roland Martinson, **Effective Youth Ministry: A Congregational Approach** *(Augsburg Fortress Publishers).*

Miles McPherson with Wayne Rice, **One Kid at a Time** *(Youth Specialties).*

Edward Sellner, **Mentoring: The Ministry of Spiritual Kinship** *(Ave Maria).*

Intensive Caring: Practical Ways to Mentor Youth *(Group Publishing).*

Successful Youth Mentoring *(Group Publishing).*

Successful Youth Mentoring 2 *(Group Publishing).*

Getting to Know You

Once a group of youth were asked how many adults in their congregation they knew well. "One." "Two or three." The responses were disappointing, but shouldn't be surprising. Typically, young people spend little time with adults in the congregation. And adults have their own activities and friendships. But you're more likely to grow in your faith when you find ways to get to know several adults who can be friends, supporters, and guides for you.

1 Read

■ Acts 2:42
■ 1 John 1:7

2 Reflect

How much time do you spend with people in your congregation?

Do you spend time socializing with members of your congregation outside of church activities?

Who are the people in your congregation who make you feel the most welcome and cared about?

3 React

In the puzzle below are twenty-four hidden words that are examples of ways people can spend time together and get to know one another in a congregation. See how many words you can find. After you find the words, use a different color to highlight the things people in your congregation do. Use a third color to highlight things you'd like to try.

P	E	E	R	M	I	N	I	S	T	R	Y	D	E	P	C
A	H	Q	S	H	S	V	Y	P	C	C	S	E	D	I	H
B	C	O	M	M	U	N	I	O	N	A	P	E	U	C	O
A	X	V	N	C	V	G	T	R	J	M	I	V	C	E	I
P	R	A	Y	E	R	I	S	T	L	P	C	E	A	C	R
T	S	Y	U	D	C	W	D	S	B	S	N	N	T	R	O
I	Y	O	U	T	H	A	C	T	I	V	I	T	I	E	S
S	F	U	N	E	R	A	L	S	S	I	C	S	O	A	M
M	C	T	B	U	U	Z	L	L	M	S	A	S	N	M	I
S	D	H	M	N	W	D	A	D	S	I	G	L	I	M	L
C	J	G	F	Y	C	E	O	V	S	T	P	V	Q	B	E
H	O	R	T	A	M	H	A	N	D	S	H	A	K	E	S
N	C	O	F	F	E	E	H	O	U	R	O	S	R	C	S
B	D	U	R	E	T	R	E	A	T	S	G	J	E	T	C
O	I	P	A	S	E	B	I	B	L	E	S	T	U	D	Y

Key:

Youth Activities	Youth Group	Hugs	Events	Sports
Education	Coffee Hour	Smiles	Ice Cream	Peer Ministry
Prayer	Visits	Handshakes	Camps	Picnic
Retreats	Phone Calls	Choir	Funerals	Bible Study
	Meals	Party	Baptisms	Communion

4 Respond

How well do you know the people in your neighborhood? at school? in activities? in other areas of your life? Choose one of these groups, and write about the ways these people take the time to get to know you—and you get to know them. Then compare this to the ways people in your congregation get to know one another. What are the differences? similarities?

STRATEGIC YOUTH MINISTRY

Involve Youth in Reaching Out to the Community

What it is

Some of the most powerful, faith-shaping experiences are those times when young people put their faith to work by serving other people. Work camps, servant events, local service projects, and personal acts of caring for others are powerful opportunities for shaping and living out the Christian faith. Indeed, Scripture is filled with calls to action to care for others, particularly those most vulnerable in the world.

As important and transforming as they may be, opportunities for service are relatively infrequent in too many congregations. Only 19 percent of LCMS youth indicate that their congregations do a good job in this area. Thus, becoming more intentional in engaging youth in meaningful acts of service is one area with tremendous untapped potential for nurturing young people's faith.

Talk with youth

■ Tell about any experiences you've had in serving other people. How did those experiences affect you, either positively or negatively?
■ What are some of your concerns about our community that could be addressed through a service project?
■ What most worries you about the thought of doing service for other people? What most excites you?

During a youth meeting, give each person a photocopy of the "Learning Together: Helping Hands and Hearts" handout on page 38. Instruct youth to work through their handouts individually, then to form pairs and share their stories with one another.

Ideas to try

■ Have youth sponsor quarterly congregation-wide outreach activities such as gathering back-to-school outfits for low-income children, decorating mitten trees at Christmas, or planting community gardens so congregational neighbors can enjoy fresh vegetables.
■ Regularly integrate mini-servant events (one day or one evening) into confirmation programs, youth group activities, and other Christian education opportunities.
■ Sponsor a snow-shoveling, window-washing, leaf-raking, or lawn-mowing afternoon for neighborhood families (nonmembers). Of course, get permission from each neighbor before you begin, emphasizing that it's a totally free service. Talk about the experience of offering your services to people you don't know.

Resources to use

Peter L. Benson and Eugene C. Roehlkepartain, **Beyond Leaf Raking: Learning to Serve/Serving to Learn** *(Abingdon Press).*

Barbara Lewis, **The Kids' Guide to Service Projects** *(Free Spirit Publishing).*

Steve Case and Fred Cornforth, **Hands-On Service Ideas for Youth Groups** *(Group Publishing).*

Eugene C. Roehlkepartain et al., **An Asset Builder's Guide to Service-Learning** *(Search Institute).*

Eugene C. Roehlkepartain, **Kids Have a Lot to Give** *(Search Institute).*

Group Workcamps *(970) 669-3836.*

Learning Together
Youth Handout

Helping Hands and Hearts

Tony is a quiet, unassuming fifteen-year-old. He rarely says a lot at church, and he's not the most popular guy around. But every week, without telling many people, he spends an afternoon at a home for young people with developmental disabilities. Not because he has to. Not because he gets school credit. But because he knows it's important, both to him and to the kids he visits. After all, they're ones who ask the director on a regular basis, "Is today a Tony day?"

Read

- Isaiah 42:1-9
- Galatians 5:13-15
- 3 John 5-8

2 Reflect

What skills or interests do you have that could benefit others in your community?

Think about a time when someone in your community was sick or needed support. What did others do for that person to help care for her or him? What else could people (including you) have done?

What kinds of things do people in your community need that they aren't already getting?

3 React

What are some of the ways you are already involved in serving your community? Write a story about a time you felt really good about your involvement with your community. What did you do? Where were you? Who else was there? How old were you? Why were you involved? How did you feel about it?

Share your story with a partner.

4 Respond

Being a part of a congregation also means being part of the larger community around that congregation. In the list below, circle the ways your congregation shows love and concern for people in the community. Add any others you can think of! Then write things you think your congregation should do. Talk to your church leaders about it.

- Serving meals to people who don't have enough food to eat
- Providing shelter for people who are homeless
- Building or repairing homes for organizations like Habitat for Humanity
- Donating money to disaster relief funds
- Donating food to community food pantries
- Holding clothing drives
- Delivering meals to people who can't leave their homes
- Visiting people who are sick
- Visiting people who are unable to leave their homes
- Collecting money for UNICEF or other organizations
- Hosting community events like concerts, plays, or festivals
- Sending representatives to community meetings
- Keeping the area around the congregation clean and free of trash

- Adopting a section of a highway and keeping it free of trash
- Sponsoring children and/or families in developing countries
- Welcoming strangers to worship and congregational activities
- Housing a daycare or nursery school program
- Offering community classes in parenting, theater, music, or other topics
- Letting others in the community use the church building for meetings or other gatherings
- Other ways your congregation shows love and concern for the community:

_____

_____

_____.

- Other ways you think your congregation can show love and concern in the future:

Section 4:

Effective
Christian Education

Effective Christian Education

If worship is the heart of congregational life, Christian education is the brain. Effective Christian education is central to whether a congregation effectively nurtures faith in young people. There are at least four dimensions to an effective Christian education program:

• An emphasis on educational content that blends theology/Bible study and life issues that are relevant to the lives of people in the group.

• Careful attention to an educational process that engages people in learning.

• Leadership that is caring, knowledgeable, and grounded in faith.

• An administrative structure of planning, evaluation, and training that undergirds all efforts.

Having a dynamite youth group or Sunday school isn't enough. Young people need to be in a congregation that effectively nurtures faith for all ages. Effective education for children lays the foundation for faith and basic Christian knowledge. Youth education provides the immediate context in which young people think about, talk about, and explore the role of faith in their lives.

And, just as important, quality adult education ensures that parents are being nurtured in their faith. Being in a congregation where many adults are stimulated and growing in faith not only models lifelong spiritual growth to youth, but also provides them with more mentors in the faith. Furthermore, when adult education is strong and adults feel nurtured, they are more willing and equipped to volunteer to lead children and youth—so that education for those ages will also be more effective.

In talking about Christian education, it's important to remember that Christian education doesn't just mean Sunday school. It also includes confirmation, youth group, Bible study groups, retreats, and dozens of other occasions where a key focus is intentionally nurturing faith.

Work Sheet 5

Evaluating Your Congregation's Christian Education

Use this work sheet to reflect on the quality of Christian education for all ages in your congregation. First, rate your congregation on each of the items in the second column. Then, list in the third column things you do to strengthen each quality. Finally, jot down other things you could do to strengthen your congregation's Christian education.

Qualities	Rating Your Congregation Needs Work = * OK = ** Great = ***	What We Do Now	What We Could Do Better
Quality Christian education for all ages	___ The congregation offers effective Christian education for children. ___ The congregation offers effective Christian education for youth. ___ The congregation offers effective Christian education for adults.		
Active involvement in Christian education	___ Most middle school youth spend at least three hours a month in Christian education. ___ Most high school youth spend at least three hours a month in Christian education.		
Interactive learning emphasis	The following regularly occur in Christian education and youth ministry: ___ Young people discuss their understanding of the Bible. ___ Young people in the class ask lots of questions. ___ Young people talk about the way they feel and think. ___ Young people talk about their faith with each other. ___ Young people talk honestly about issues and concerns in their lives.		
Excellent Bible study	___ The congregation offers excellent Bible study opportunities for youth.		
Making Scripture come alive	___ Christian education opportunities do an excellent job of making Scripture come alive for children, youth, and adults.		
Apply faith to daily life	___ Christian education opportunities emphasize helping young people apply their faith to their daily lives.		

Provide Quality Christian Education for All Ages

What it is

Christian education is like a three-legged stool: All three legs need to be strong for it to be a quality stool. In Christian education, the program only performs optimally when it is strong for all three major age groups: children, youth, and adults. From a youth ministry perspective, if the children's education isn't strong, young people do not have an adequate foundation upon which to grow during adolescence. If adult education isn't strong, the youth program struggles with spiritually undernourished volunteers and parents who aren't equipped to be faith models and educators for their children.

The emerging challenge for congregations is to focus energy on developing high-quality Christian education for all ages so that each age group supports and reinforces the others. Until that happens, the Christian education program for youth will struggle.

Talk with youth

■ If you were involved in the church as a child, what parts of Sunday school or other Christian education activities do you remember most fondly? What parts didn't interest you or help you grow?

■ What would you say are the strengths of our Christian education program for youth? What are things you'd like to see changed?

Ideas to try

■ Develop goals and objectives for your education for all ages based on your congregation's vision and mission (see Key 23). Use these as guides when selecting curriculum and developing lesson plans.

■ Each year evaluate your congregation's Christian education programming. Ask people what's working and what could be improved.

■ Offer regular teacher training workshops in which teachers gain new skills and learn from each other.

Resources to use

Charles R. Foster, **Educating Congregations: The Future of Christian Education** *(Abingdon Press).*

Karl Leuthauser, **Character Counts!: 40 Youth Ministry Devotions From Extraordinary Christians** *(Group Publishing).*

Eugene C. Roehlkepartain, **The Teaching Church: Moving Christian Education to Center Stage** *(Abingdon Press).*

Thom and Joani Schultz, **The Dirt on Learning** *(Group Publishing).*

Encourage Ongoing Involvement in Christian Education

What it is

Almost every survey shows the same thing: When young people move from middle school to high school, many of them "drop out" of Christian education. The levels of involvement continue to decline so that only a small portion of adults in most congregations are regularly involved in Christian education.

Christian education can be a powerful experience for all ages...but not if people don't participate. Because there is a widespread belief that "Christian education is for children," extra effort is needed to keep older youth and adults actively involved.

Keeping both groups involved is important for youth ministry. If older youth drop out, they're less likely to develop lifelong commitments to the church, and they're more likely to turn elsewhere for help as they face difficult questions about life and the world. And one reason youth may drop out is that they see that most adults—including their parents—have dropped out.

Encouraging ongoing involvement requires at least two things. First, it requires having opportunities for involvement that are relevant and engaging. Second, it requires changing expectations so that people know it is important—and enriching—to stay involved.

Resources to use

Thom and Joani Schultz, **Why Nobody Learns Much of Anything at Church: And How to Fix It** *(Group Publishing).*

Thom and Joani Schultz, **The Dirt on Learning** *(Group Publishing).*

Lyle E. Schaller, **44 Ways to Expand the Teaching Ministry of Your Church** *(Abingdon Press).*

Talk with youth

■ In what ways does this congregation encourage youth to stay involved in Christian education? In what ways does it hinder ongoing involvement?

■ What kinds of activities, topics, or opportunities would make you most eager to continue participating in Christian education throughout high school?

Ideas to try

■ Shift the language, subtle messages, and expectations that make people think Christian education equals children's education. Make it clear that lifelong learning is important for Christian discipleship.

■ Offer interesting and challenging opportunities for youth after they have been confirmed. Include opportunities for leadership and service.

■ Call on young people who are no longer active in the youth group or other congregational activities. Find out why they have become less active.

Use Interactive Learning Methods

What it is

Suppose you want to learn how to tie a knot. You go to a class, and the instructor tells you all about the ins and outs of knot-tying. You go home, ready to tie the knot, but you never can get it quite right. So you call a neighbor, who comes over to help. She gives you a rope, then guides you through it step by step. After a couple of tries, you have a great knot, and, best of all, you remember how to do it!

The illustration is a bit absurd, but it makes a point: Too often in Christian education, we tell people a lot about faith and beliefs, but we don't give them time to "try things out" or really experience what we're telling them.

Rather than focusing on the leader telling students everything they ought or need to know, interactive learning involves the give-and-take that helps young people test their ideas and learn from each other. It helps them grow by guiding them to connect their real-life experiences with their faith.

True, leaders in an interactive style of learning do not have as much control. Students will say things that don't make sense or may seem heretical. But the other side is that they will also discover insightful, meaningful things that they— and others—will remember long after they have forgotten a well-crafted lecture.

Resources to use

Bill McNabb and Steve Mabry, **Teaching the Bible Creatively** *(Youth Specialties).*

Thom and Joani Schultz, **Do It! Active Learning in Youth Ministry** *(Group Publishing).*

Talk with youth

■ What kinds of learning opportunities do you most often experience in this congregation: ones that involve a lot of sitting and listening to other people or ones that involve more involvement by class members?

■ What types of opportunities do you most enjoy? Which ones are most challenging? Which ones help you grow the most in your faith?

During a youth meeting, give each person a photocopy of the "Learning Together: What's Your Learning Style?" handout on page 45. Instruct youth to form groups of three, and have partners work through their handouts together.

When groups have finished the exercises on their handouts, ask each group to share its ideas from the "Respond" section on the handout. As groups call out ideas, list them on newsprint.

Ideas to try

■ As an experiment, keep track of how much you talk during a class and how much students participate. Reflect on what you learn and its implications for your teaching.

■ Offer workshops for teachers and youth group leaders about interactive learning. Give them opportunities to simulate and practice leading interactive classes.

■ Select curricula and meeting planning resources that include activities, simulations, role-plays, discussions, and other forms of interaction.

■ Develop a resource library that includes resources for teachers and youth group leaders on interactive or active learning.

Learning Together
Youth Handout
What's Your Learning Style?

What's your all-time favorite class in school? Now think about what happens (or used to happen) in that class. You probably liked the subject matter. But one of the reasons you learned the material probably related to the types of activities and discussions you had. The best way to learn things is to get actively involved in them. The same is true at church. You're more likely to learn about the Bible, theology, and their meaning for your life if you don't just listen to lectures, but if you interact with other people and participate in activities in the congregation.

Read

■ Jeremiah 19:1-13
■ Matthew 13:1-13
■ Acts 8:26-40

2 Reflect

■ What are some of the ways people in the Bible used to teach, based on the Scripture passages listed?

■ Who are the teachers who have taught you the most in your life? Why were you able to learn so much from them? Did they lecture a lot? tell stories? lead discussions? assign a lot of homework? use games and other activities?

■ What can you do to help make classes and groups in your church more interactive? (For example, asking questions when you have the opportunity.)

3 React

One way to learn with and from others is for several people to read something and then talk about your different interpretations and perspectives—rather than having just one person tell you the "right" answers!

Try this exercise: With your group members, select a Bible passage you're all familiar with. Feel free to read it over to refresh your memory. Then each of you write a summary of your interpretation of that passage. Who are the key people? What happened to the people in the story? What are the key messages? (Don't worry about getting the "right" answers!)

When everyone is finished, exchange summaries with your partners in your group. Compare the three summaries, yours and theirs. Are the summaries all exactly the same? Discuss the differences and similarities with your partners.

4 Respond

Create a list for youth group leaders, Sunday school teachers, and others in your church of what kinds of classes are most interesting to you. Propose specific ways you can work with them to think of ways to make classes more interactive and engaging.

_____

_____

_____

Key 14

Offer Excellent Bible Study

What it is

K ey 13 emphasized how to teach; Key 14 focuses more on what to teach. No amount of creative, interactive education will be adequate if not combined with an emphasis on excellent Bible study. This involves more than just using Scripture for occasional proof texts. It involves engaging youth actively in studying Scripture.

One of the dangers in dividing process (Key 13) and content (Key 14) is that they seem separate from each other. But excellent Bible study is best achieved when it uses the kinds of interactive learning styles that draw young people into an active dialogue with Scripture.

Talk with youth

■ Tell about the time you have most enjoyed studying Scripture. What was it about that experience that made it so meaningful to you?

■ What parts of Scripture are most confusing or puzzling to you? What are areas of the Bible about which you'd like to learn more?

Ideas to try

■ When studying Scripture with youth, work to make connections between Scripture and their everyday lives. Show ways that the Bible can be relevant and meaningful to them.

■ Offer youth leaders additional training in understanding Scripture so they are more comfortable leading discussions with youth about Scripture.

■ Encourage youth Sunday school and Bible study leaders to participate in training programs such as LifeLight, Crossways, Bethel Bible Series, Serendipity, and others.

Resources to use

Bill McNabb and Steve Mabry, **Teaching the Bible Creatively** *(Youth Specialties).*

The Youth Worker's Encyclopedia of Bible-Teaching Ideas: Old Testament and New Testament *(Group Publishing).*

Key 15

Teach the Bible in Ways That Make It Come Alive for Youth

What it is

In *Transforming Bible Study*, Walter Wink identifies three elements of a discussion about Scripture that can help it come alive:

1. Critical issues—Understanding the text and its context. Whereas this stage is often addressed in a mini-lecture format, Wink suggests that it is more powerful for people to ask questions and look together in resource guides (such as commentaries) for the answers.

2. Amplification—This stage involves getting into the story of the passage, "where we try to live into the narrative until it becomes vivid for us." This can be done by role playing, miming, or other approaches. "Only as the text comes alive for us can we attempt to hear again the question that occasioned the answer provided by the text," Wink contends.

3. Application—Finally, once young people have entered the world of the Scripture, they are ready to look for contemporary meaning and relevance. Wink puts it this way: "It is not enough to understand the text intellectually, or to see certain parallels with our own condition. We need to let it move deeply within us" (pp. 38-39).

Resources to use

The Youth Bible *(New Century Version, Group Publishing).*

Dean W. Nadasdy, **Cross Views: Story Dramas That Teach the Faith** *(Concordia Publishing House).*

Walter Wink, **Transforming Bible Study, Second Edition** *(Abingdon Press).*

Living Beyond Belief *(Group Publishing).*

Talk with youth

■ What parts of Scripture are most "real" to you? What brought them alive for you?

■ What character in Scripture do you think you are most like? What can that character teach you?

During a youth meeting, give each person a photocopy of the "Learning Together: Real Life" handout on pages 48-49. Instruct youth to form groups of three, and have partners work through their handouts together.

Ideas to try

■ Invite several church members to talk with youth about the different ways they read and study Scripture. Use the differences in approaches to highlight to youth the importance of finding a style that fits them.

■ Experiment with different ways of studying Scripture. Use drama, role-plays, debates, guided reflections, and other approaches. Then reflect on the experiences to determine which approaches are most helpful and meaningful to youth in your congregation.

■ Encourage youth to use a Bible translation that they can understand. Some of the easiest translations to understand include the New Century Version (Word Publishing), the Contemporary English Version (American Bible Society), and the New Living Translation (Tyndale House Publishers).

Learning Together
Youth Handout

Real Life

War…Romance…Adventure…Drama…Mystery. Those words might be used by marketers to sell a hot new movie or novel. But they could also be used to describe the Bible. Why? Because those things are part of real life, and the Bible is filled with real life. Sometimes we forget we're reading about far away places and times long ago. But taking time to read and learn Scripture can make the Bible be a story for you and a guide for real life.

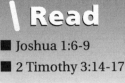

Read

- Joshua 1:6-9
- 2 Timothy 3:14-17

---

2 Reflect

■ How often do you spend time thinking about or reading the Bible? How do you feel about the amount of time you spend?

■ Do you think reading and studying Scripture is an important part of being a faithful person? Why or why not?

■ When Scripture is read during worship services, do you usually listen and understand the messages? Do you think Scripture readings are an important part of worship?

3 React

Think about the books you read for fun or relaxation. Are they action/adventure stories? romances? dramas? Do you read stories from the Bible for fun?

The Bible is made up of many different kinds of stories. Below are different types of stories. In your group, try to think of one story in the Bible that fits in each category. In the boxes below, write the chapter and verse numbers with a title beside the type of story. Then write a brief summary or draw a picture representing the story. Then read the stories you picked!

Action/Adventure:	Summary or Picture:

Romance:	Summary or Picture:

STRATEGIC YOUTH MINISTRY

Drama:	Summary or Picture:

Biography:	Summary or Picture:

Mystery:	Summary or Picture:

Comedy:	Summary or Picture:

↵ Respond

Try spending twenty minutes by yourself, reading a favorite Bible passage (or one you pick at random). After twenty minutes, summarize what you read. Then write about your experience. Did you like reading the Bible by yourself? Did you understand what you read? What questions do you have about it? What experiences in your own life did it remind you of? If you have trouble with this activity, talk with a pastor or youth leader about finding a Bible and some study tools that make the Bible easier to understand.

Emphasize Connections Between Faith and Life

What it is

It's easy for faith to become a church-only thing. At church, young people spend time with other people who share their values and perspectives. They talk about faith openly, because it is expected and natural. But when they leave the church, it's not always so easy. In other places—even at home, sometimes—it's easy to forget what you've learned about your faith when you're struggling to fit in or to impress others. It's hard to do things differently because of your faith.

Thus, congregations have an important role in helping youth see their faith as integrated into all areas of their lives: their homes, their schools, their work, their romantic relationships, their future. When young people see—and live— the connections, their faith can come alive and shape everything they do.

Talk with youth

■ When has your faith been a resource to you in your everyday life? What did you learn from that experience?

■ What are the areas of your life that seem most removed from your faith and congregational life? What's separating them? What could help draw them together?

During a youth meeting, give each person a photocopy of the "Learning Together: Decisions, Decisions" handout on pages 51-52. Instruct youth to work through their handouts individually, then to complete the "Respond" section in small groups.

Ideas to try

■ Give youth plenty of opportunities to talk about what's happening in their lives. Guide them in making connections between their everyday questions and concerns, and their faith.

■ Invite adult members of the congregation to talk with the youth group about how they connect their faith to their profession. Include a variety of vocations, including businesspeople, doctors, lawyers, human services workers, teachers, and computer specialists.

■ Get to know your young people's world so you can help them make connections between their world and their faith. Regularly eat lunch with youth at the school cafeteria (be sure it's OK with the school).

Resources to use

Shock Wave Video Series *(Group Publishing).*

Duffy Robbins, **The Ministry of Nurture: How to Build Real Life Faith Into Your Kids** *(Youth Specialties).*

Merton Strommen, Charles Bruning, and Dick Hardel, **FaithTalk** *(Augsburg Youth and Family Institute).*

Learning Together
Youth Handout

Decisions, Decisions

Every day, you make thousands of little—and big—decisions. You may not think of it much, but your faith can make a difference in what you do—and don't do. Should you take time to talk with a lonely friend when you're in a hurry to get home? How does your faith help you sort out whether to take a particular after-school job? By helping you apply your faith to these real-life decisions, your congregation is helping you grow in your faith.

Read

- Deuteronomy 30:11-20
- Jeremiah 17:5-8
- Luke 16:19-31

2 Reflect

■ Think about a difficult decision you've made. What was your process? Did you ask yourself questions? Did you make a list of pros and cons for each choice you could make? Did you pray about it?

■ What role does your faith play in your decision-making process? How do prayer, Bible study, your beliefs, and other dimensions of your faith help you make good decisions?

■ What do these Bible passages tell us about the way we make decisions in our daily lives?

3 React

Our faith plays a role in every decision we make, even when we don't realize it. Sometimes we choose to ignore our faith when we have an important decision. Sometimes we pray and study Scripture to seek guidance. Other times we look to members of our congregation and to our beliefs to help us make choices. Think about three decisions you have made in the past month. Write about the role that your faith played in helping you make each of those decisions. Draw a face that illustrates how you feel about the choice you made. What might you change the next time?

Decision	How My Faith Influenced My Decision	How I Feel About My Faith	What I Might Change

Decision	How My Faith Influenced My Decision	How I Feel About My Faith	What I Might Change

⚲ Respond

In your group, list the kinds of decisions you make (both the big ones and the little ones). Identify those where you would most value help and support from the congregation. Then talk with leaders about ways to get guidance in those areas.

_____

_____

_____

_____

_____

_____

_____

Section 5:

Evangelism and Mission Emphasis

Evangelism and Mission Emphasis

For much of this century, most congregations have employed the following five methods of evangelism, according to American Baptist pastor C. Jeff Woods:

• holding crusades or mass meetings where the basic goal is to encourage people to make a commitment to Christ,

• relying on families in the church to replenish their congregation with new members,

• developing quality programs that are designed to attract new people,

• visiting people door to door, and

• waiting for newcomers to show up.

Woods believes that none of these kinds of evangelism are adequate today. Instead, he writes, it's time for congregations to adopt a style of relational evangelism in which people share "the good news about Jesus Christ with someone you already care about and to whom you have already demonstrated God's love." This approach, he contends, "has become the primary way that people come to hear the Gospel."[3]

If Woods is accurate, congregations have a great deal of work to do to prepare young people and adults to contribute to this relational approach to evangelism. Many people in congregations are not comfortable talking about their faith with each other—much less sharing their journeys of faith to those who do not share their beliefs.

There's another reason to emphasize evangelism and missions: When congregations do it, a side-effect is that youth (and adults) are more likely to be growing in their faith. Why? Perhaps one reason is that people are challenged to grow in their own faith as they think about sharing that faith with others.

Work Sheet 6

Evaluating Your Congregation's Evangelism and Mission Emphasis

Use this work sheet to reflect on how your congregation emphasizes missions and evangelism. First, rate your congregation on each of the items in the second column. Then, list in the third column things you already do to strengthen each quality. Finally, jot down other things you could do to strengthen your congregation's missions and evangelism emphasis.

Qualities	Rating Your Congregation Needs Work = * OK = ** Great = ***	What We Do Now	What We Could Do Better
Emphasis on evangelism and missions	___ The congregation emphasizes bringing the gospel to people outside the church. ___ The congregation makes missions (domestic and international) and evangelism important in congregational life.		
Emphasis on personal sharing	___ The congregation strengthens young people's ability to talk about Christ with others.		

Emphasize Evangelism and Missions in the Youth Program

What it is

To youth, missions can seem so distant and removed. Yet an emphasis on missions in the congregation can also expand young people's horizons and get them deeply interested in the world and their place in it. Thus, a missions emphasis in the congregation and the youth program can enrich the youth program by exposing youth to different cultures and ways of life.

While missions can seem distant, evangelism (the close-to-home expression of missions) can seem scary and awkward. Most youth are still trying to figure out their own faith. Talking about that faith with others can be quite threatening or intimidating.

Perhaps the combination of missions seeming distant and evangelism seeming threatening has led many congregations to underemphasize them in their youth ministries. Yet recovering this emphasis can give new energy to young people's faith as they learn to articulate it for others and learn how their faith is being shared around the world.

- -

Resources to use

Ridge Burns and Noel Becchetti, **The Complete Student Missions Handbook** *(Youth Specialties).*

George G. Hunter III, **Church for the Unchurched** *(Abingdon Press).*

Alan C. Klass, **In Search of the Unchurched: Why People Don't Join Your Congregation** *(Alban Institute).*

Talk with youth

■ When you think about missions and evangelism, what words and feelings come to you?

■ What are some places in our own community where people need to hear the good news of the gospel? How can we be bearers of this good news?

■ What are your biggest fears or areas of discomfort with evangelism and missions? What would help you overcome those fears and the discomfort?

Ideas to try

■ Provide nonthreatening opportunities for young people to bring friends with them to church, then have follow-up opportunities where these friends can get to know other youth and hear the good news.

■ Encourage the youth group to adopt another youth group in a mission field. Develop pen pals for sharing and relationship building. Do service projects (such as gathering supplies) to assist the partner youth group.

■ Have youth sponsor a developing country Christmas bazaar that allows members to purchase Christmas gifts from countries where your church sponsors missionaries.

■ Provide firsthand experiences in missions by sponsoring workcamps and mission trips to both domestic and international locations.

Teach Youth to Share Their Faith With Others

What it is

When we talk about sharing our faith with others, we often have images of door-to-door evangelists and dramatic, inspiring "testimonies." While those are certainly some of the ways people share their faith, the most common experiences are much less dramatic—and much less scary.

Young people, as well as adults, need to become comfortable with telling their faith stories to others in their daily lives. When they're talking to their friends in the school cafeteria. When they're sitting in the living room watching television with their parents. When they're talking about the Bible during Sunday school or confirmation.

Sharing our faith with others isn't a matter of mastering theological concepts or being able to answer every question. It's a matter of finding the words to express how faith has had an impact on their lives. In some ways, it's not much different from telling someone about a special friend.

In addition to the skills involved in sharing their faith, young people also need a safe and affirming place where they can begin telling their story without fear of being laughed at. Creating such a climate of trust and affirmation is an important challenge for congregations.

Resources to use

Robert J. McCarty, **Teen to Teen: Responding to Peers in Crisis** *(St. Mary's Press).*

Core Belief Bible Study Series: Why Sharing Faith Matters *(Group Publishing).*

Core Belief Bible Study Series: The Truth About Sharing Faith *(Group Publishing).*

Talk with youth

■ When you think of "sharing your faith" with others, what images or experiences come to mind, both positive and negative?

■ When, if ever, have you shared your faith story with others? What was it like? What happened? What did you learn about yourself and your faith?

■ What are the different ways you can share your faith with others?

During a youth meeting, give each person a photocopy of the "Learning Together: Telling the Good News" handout on page 58. Instruct youth to find partners they know well and trust and then to complete their handouts in pairs.

Ideas to try

■ Offer classes in faith-sharing skills for youth through Sunday school, youth group, or midweek activities.

■ Invite adults in the congregation to share their faith stories with youth. Be sure to include adults who don't "have all the answers" so youth realize that they don't have to be perfect to share their faith. Also include adults who don't have dramatic testimonies to share.

■ Incorporate opportunities for youth to share their own faith stories during Christian education classes, confirmation, camping experiences, and youth group meetings. Make it a natural part of your youth ministry.

Learning Together
Youth Handout
Telling the Good News

Usually when we have some good news, we want to tell everyone. We call all our friends. And we can barely hold it in if it's supposed to be a surprise. But when it comes to sharing the good news of our faith, many people barely get it out. It's hard. It's awkward. Somehow it seems like this good news is not like other good news.

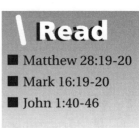

Read
- Matthew 28:19-20
- Mark 16:19-20
- John 1:40-46

2 Reflect

- How comfortable are you telling others about your beliefs?
- What do these Bible passages tell you about the importance of talking to others about your faith?
- In what ways, if any, does your congregation help you share your faith with others?
- What more could your congregation do to help you?

3 React

Information and messages come from many different sources all the time. Think about the different places you get information such as radio, television, parents, friends, church, movies, and advertisements. What kinds of messages are they sending you? Which ones do you listen to? Why?

Now think about the messages you give to others. Specifically, what kinds of messages do you give about your faith? Do you talk to your friends about your beliefs? to family members? to strangers? Think about these issues as you answer the questions below.

What do I want to tell others about my faith?

_____

What are some ways besides talking that I share my faith with others?

_____

How can I share my faith in ways that people will listen and pay attention to?

_____

Is it important to let others know what I believe? Why or why not?

_____

4 Respond

One of the best ways to share your faith with others is to tell them about how faith has been important in your life. Take time to write down your own faith journey—both its ups and downs. Then share your story with your partner. Later, when you have a chance to share your faith with someone you don't know as well, it won't be so hard.

Section 6:

Inspiring Worship for Youth

Inspiring Worship for Youth

Worship is the heart of congregational life, and it can also be an important influence on young people's growth in faith. Yet while adults typically rank worship as a strength in their congregation, young people are much less likely to do so. For about half of the young people surveyed, worship is a dull ritual that has little to do with their lives, rather than a renewing experience that nurtures their souls and challenges their minds.

For some youth workers, worship is a nonissue. Worship is the pastor's responsibility, not a youth ministry function. But here's the reality: More young people experience weekly worship than any other youth activity in a typical congregation. Thus, young people's experiences of worship have the potential to be an important source of spiritual nourishment. Or it can dull their interest in the spiritual and push them away because of boredom.

Many people debate whether "inspiring worship" is, by definition, a particular type of worship such as contemporary worship. But that may not be the most important question. Regardless of the style of worship in a congregation, the quality of the worship experience appears to be much more important. Kennon L. Callahan suggests five factors that make a difference in the quality of the worship experience, regardless of the particular style:

1. The warmth and winsomeness of the service and the congregation.

2. Dynamic and inspiring music.

3. Quality preaching that is easy to follow, relevant, and engaging.

4. A liturgy in which each element builds on the others like a drama.

5. A sanctuary that is comfortably full.[4]

Youth workers cannot guarantee that young people will experience all of these factors in the congregation's worship service. But they can work with worship leaders, youth, and other congregation members to ensure that young people's interests, developmental needs, and faith journeys are considered as worship services are planned and led in the congregation.

Evaluating Your Congregation's Worship Experiences for Youth

Use this work sheet to reflect on how youth experience worship in your congregation. First, rate your congregation on each of the items in the second column. Then, in the third column list things you already do to strengthen each quality. Finally, jot down other things you could do to strengthen your congregation's worship experiences for youth.

Qualities	Rating Your Congregation Needs Work = * OK = ** Great = ***	What We Do Now	What We Could Do Better
Strong preaching	___ Young people get a lot out of sermons during worship services.		
Meaningful worship	___ Young people get a lot out of worship services.		

Published in *Strategic Youth Ministry* by Group Publishing, Inc., P.O. Box 481, Loveland, CO 80539.

Make Sermons Relevant to Youth

What it is

The great contemporary preacher John Killinger writes about the sermon: "It is not a twenty-minute space in the liturgy merely to be filled with my talk. It is an opportunity within the orchestration of the divine service to speak for Christ in the most imaginative, communicative way possible, so that the Holy Spirit finds the situation combustible and can truly ignite the hearts of the congregation."[5]

What would have to happen in sermons to "truly ignite the hearts" of youth in congregations? How would the sermons be different? You could probably comb the shelves of the local Christian bookstore before finding any "homiletic helps" that specifically address those questions. But if youth are an important part of the congregation, then it's essential that pastors be encouraged to explore these kinds of questions. In the same way that pastors often direct a sermon or a story or a theme to senior citizens or parents who fill the pews, why not do the same for youth?

Resources to use

Mike and Amy Nappa, **Bore No More!** *(Group Publishing).*

Bore No More! 2 *(Group Publishing).*

Talk with youth

■ What is the most memorable sermon you have ever heard? What was it about that sermon that made it so memorable to you?

■ What are some things you'd like to hear about in sermons? What are some concerns or needs in your world for which you need the kind of guidance and support that can come through sermons?

During a youth meeting, give each person a photocopy of the "Learning Together: Qualities of a Good Sermon" handout on pages 63-64. Instruct youth to complete their handouts on their own.

Ideas to try

■ Invite your pastor to attend a youth group meeting to talk about what goes into preparing and preaching a sermon.

■ Take youth to worship services in congregations of other traditions, particularly those with a variety of preaching styles. (Or get videotapes of the services to watch the sermons during a youth group event.) Talk about the different styles, why different traditions have different styles, and what features of different styles appeal to different people.

■ For at least four weeks in a row, have the pastor meet weekly with a group of youth to talk about the next sermon and how it can address their needs and interests.

Learning Together
Youth Handout

Qualities of a Good Sermon

A Baylor University survey of preaching experts identified qualities of great sermons. Some of the qualities they identified included these:

- *They do a good job of interpreting Scripture.*
- *They are relevant to everyday life.*
- *They reflect the preacher's life experiences and faith commitment.*
- *They clearly communicate through simple language and illustrations.*
- *They are well-organized and focused.*

Which of these is most important to you?

1 Read

■ Jonah 3:1-10
■ Matthew 5–7
■ Mark 1:4-8

- -

2 Reflect

■ In what ways do the "sermons" in these Scripture passages reflect (or contradict) the qualities identified by preaching experts?

■ In a sermon what communicates best to you? Is it a clear interpretation of Scripture? a sense of humor? lots of stories? practical ideas of what you can do?

■ What are things you can do to get more out of the sermons at church?

3 React

It's important for pastors to know what young people think and feel about their sermons. Write your ideas for things you'd like to hear your pastor preach about and elements you like and dislike in sermons. Then share them with your pastor. If you don't feel comfortable talking directly to your pastor, share your ideas with a youth worker or another adult.

4 Respond

Sometimes one of the keys to getting a lot out of sermons is learning how to listen to them. Use this work sheet during a sermon to help you understand what the preacher wants to communicate. Make copies of this sheet so you can keep notes on sermons in the future.

Sermon Title:	Date Preached:
Scripture Text(s):	By:

Key Points:	
Memorable Quotes or Stories:	
Questions I Still Have:	
What It Means for Me:	Actions to Take in Response:

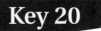

Offer Meaningful Worship for Youth

What it is

"Sunday worship in the average congregation is R-rated," writes United Methodist pastor Stephen P. West. "It is for adults only."[6] Sometimes we assume that youth will be bored in worship. But it doesn't have to be that way. Many worship leaders find that worship becomes more meaningful to youth when…

• worship is experiential, involving youth (and the rest of the congregation) in responsive singing, reading, and praying.

• youth have opportunities to assist or lead in worship through choir, special music, Scripture readings, drama, and other opportunities.

• worship leaders always plan the services keeping in mind that young people will be participating and listening. This filter can help with selecting hymns that young people know, focusing a sermon, and selecting key points and stories to include in the sermon.

Talk with youth

■ What is the most meaningful part of worship for you? What part is most boring? What makes these elements either meaningful or boring to you?

■ If you were asked to develop a worship service just for youth, what parts of a typical service would you keep the way they are? What parts would you change, and why?

■ What are some ways to help you concentrate and get something out of worship services in your congregation?

During a youth meeting, give each person a photocopy of the "Learning Together: What Lifts You Up?" hand-out on pages 66-67. Instruct youth to form groups of three to five people and complete their handouts together.

Ideas to try

■ Involve youth as readers, cast members in skits, members of choirs and other musical groups, and participants in other leadership capacities that make worship more meaningful for them and their peers.

■ In a youth group meeting, have young people brainstorm about all the ways they could be involved in the worship service. Together, choose the best ideas, then work with the pastor to begin implementing some of them.

■ Plan an annual youth Sunday. Have youth plan the entire service. Take this opportunity as a chance to deepen young people's experiences in and understanding of worship.

■ Use a variety of musical styles and mediums (drama, dance, responsive readings, dialogue sermons, multimedia presentations) to keep people of all ages involved and interested.

Resources to use

Worship Ideas for Youth Ministry *(Group Publishing).*

Worship Ideas for Youth Ministry 2 *(Group Publishing).*

No More Us & Them: 100 Ways to Bring Your Youth & Church Together *(Group Publishing).*

Terry Dittmer, **Creating Contemporary Worship** *(LCMS Department of Youth Ministry).*

Learning Together
Youth Handout

What Lifts You Up?

Why do you attend worship services? Because you have to? Because everyone else does? Theologians say that people participate in worship solely to glorify God. In addition, however, worship can have a profound effect on the worshipper. Worship can lift your spirit and open your mind, heart, and soul to God's presence and calling.

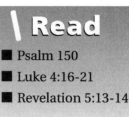

\ Read

■ Psalm 150

■ Luke 4:16-21

■ Revelation 5:13-14

ʹ2 Reflect

■ In what ways are the worship services in your congregation like or unlike the worship experiences described in these Bible passages?

■ Name one of the most uplifting worship experiences you've had.

■ If you planned worship services in your congregation, what elements of your current services would you keep and what would you change? How?

ʹ3 React

Think about all the reasons you attend worship services: Your parents want you to go; you like the time to celebrate and express your faith; your friends go; you like the music; you feel a strong commitment to regular worship and giving thanks.

People attend church services for many different reasons. Of course, not all the reasons apply to everyone. Below and on the following page, make a list of ten reasons you attend worship services. Write your list first, then number them in order of priority (1=the reason you most often have for attending; 10=the reason you least often have for attending). Then compare them to the lists of other people in your group.

Rank	Reason

Rank	Reason

⌖ Respond

Do you usually attend worship services for your own fulfillment or to please someone else? Over the next three months, concentrate on your reasons for attending services. Focus on the elements of worship that are important to your faith. As you think of these things, write them down. Then, when you don't really feel like getting up for church one morning, or you feel like someone is making you go, remember what you wrote about worship that is important to you.

Section 7:

Support for Families

Support for Families

There's little debate about the importance of the family in shaping young people's lives, including their physical, intellectual, emotional, psychological, and social development. But we sometimes forget that the family is just as important in the area of spiritual or faith development. In fact, a family has more influence on a young person's growth in faith than anything that happens in a congregation or youth ministry.

The *Congregations at Crossroads* study measured several ways that families express faith in the home. Four dynamics are particularly important (both in childhood and in adolescence):

1. Talking about faith with your mother.
2. Talking about faith with your father.
3. Having family devotions or prayer.
4. Doing family projects to help other people.

Relatively few parents receive a lot of guidance from their congregations in knowing how to nurture faith in their children. It's clear that parents—particularly fathers—would benefit from congregations that emphasize parent education and support as part of their youth program (or their youth and family ministry). The efforts will have a direct benefit in the growth in faith of the young people themselves.

Work Sheet 8

Evaluating Your Congregation's Support for Parents

Use this work sheet to reflect on how your congregation supports parents. First, rate your congregation on each of the items in the second column. Then, list in the third column things you already do to strengthen each quality. Finally, jot down other things you could do to strengthen your congregation's support for parents.

Qualities	Rating Your Congregation Needs Work = * OK = ** Great = ***	What We Do Now	What We Could Do Better
Strengthening family life	___The congregation does a good or excellent job strengthening family life.		
Parent education	The congregation helps parents learn how to nurture the faith of their children through… ___ conversations between children and their fathers about faith issues. ___ conversations between children and their mothers about faith issues. ___ family devotions or prayer. ___ family projects to help other people.		

Make Strengthening Family Life a Priority of Youth Ministry

What it is

In 1990 Search Institute released a major study of eleven thousand youth and adults in mainline Protestant churches. That study found that what happens in families has as much or more influence on young people's faith than anything that happens in the congregation. Yet fewer than one in four congregations actively work to strengthen families in nurturing faith.[7]

What does it mean for youth ministry to make strengthening family life a priority? It means, in the words of Christian educator Ben Freudenburg, "a shift from church-centered, home-supported [youth] ministry to home-centered, church-supported ministry."[8] It means building a youth program (and congregational life) around the needs of families, rather than expecting families to shape their lives around the needs of the congregation.

Talk with youth

■ What things happen in our congregation that tell you that families are important? What things happen that indicate that families may not be very important?

■ What happens at church that gets in the way of spending time with your family?

■ What kinds of things would you like to do that might help you feel more comfortable talking about faith issues with your parents?

Ideas to try

■ Plan activities that intentionally draw families together rather than pull them apart. For example, start a Wednesday evening family meal before education classes and choir. And make your choir a "family choir," not a youth choir or an adult choir.

■ Hold a regular meeting for parents to talk about shared goals for nurturing faith in young people. Ask them about their expectations of the congregation and discuss the congregation's expectations of them. Share areas where families need the congregation's support and the congregation needs the support of families.

Resources to use

Mark DeVries, **Family-Based Youth Ministry** *(InterVarsity Press).*

Richard Olson and Joe Leonard, **A New Day for Family Ministry** *(Alban Institute).*

130 Ways to Involve Parents in Youth Ministry *(Group Publishing).*

Irene Strommen, **Faith and Skills for Parenting** *(Youth and Family Institute of Augsburg College).*

Equip Parents to Nurture Faith in Their Children

What it is

The Search Institute study of LCMS congregations identified at least four ways families nurture faith. Here are percentages of the youth surveyed who say they often experience these activities at home between the ages of thirteen and eighteen:

• Talk with mother about faith: 30 percent

• Talk with father about faith: 16 percent

• Have family devotions or prayer at home: 16 percent

• Have family projects in which we help other people: 8 percent

These statistics suggest some specific areas where congregations could usefully put energy into equipping parents to nurture faith in their children.

- -

Talk with youth

■ In what ways do your parents guide your faith and beliefs? What do they do that has helped you the most?

■ What makes it awkward to talk about faith and church with your parents? What might make it easier?

During a youth meeting, give each person a photocopy of the "Learning Together: Family Faith" handout on page 74. Instruct youth to form groups of three to five and complete their handouts in their groups.

Ideas to try

■ Concentrate energy on helping fathers get more involved in talking about faith and life issues with their children and teenagers. Give them practice in talking about their own faith and experiences so they'll be more comfortable talking about these things with their children.

■ If you don't have it already, start a Christian education class for parents on Sunday mornings when their children are involved in their own classes. Focus on equipping parents in their role as faith nurturers. Also explore the possibility of a similar class for parents while their children are in confirmation programs.

■ Hold a parent-youth retreat during which you have separate sessions for parents and youth to learn faith-nurturing skills. Then provide opportunities to try the skills out on someone else's parent or child. Finally, participants can use the skills with their own parent or child.

Resources to use

Ben Freudenburg with Rick Lawrence, **The Family-Friendly Church** (Group Publishing).

It Takes More Than Love video series (Seraphim Communication).

David Lynn, **Parent Ministry Talksheets** (Youth Specialties).

Jolene L. Roehlkepartain, **Ideas for Parents Newsletters Master Set** (Search Institute).

Learning Together
Youth Handout

Family Faith

Though we sometimes think faith is a "church thing," your family life has more influence on your faith than anything that happens at church. Congregations can do a lot of things to make it easier to grow in faith through your family. These may include offering suggestions for family activities focused on faith, providing opportunities for families to do things together, and helping parents and youth communicate better. How does your congregation help your family?

1 Read
- Genesis 25:19-34
- Genesis 37:1-36

---

2 Reflect

■ The families in these Bible passages didn't have very healthy ways of dealing with their problems and disagreements. What are some of the ways your family deals with difficult situations? What role does faith play in those times?

■ What are some ways your family nurtures your faith?

■ How does your congregation help your family apply your faith to family life?

■ What other ways could your congregation help your family focus more attention on growing in faith at home?

3 React

Work with your group to think of some of the ways your congregation helps families nurture faith. Write the general idea in the left column and specific examples in the right column.

Ways my congregation help families nurture faith	Examples
Example: Helps families learn how to study the Bible together.	Offers Monday night parent/teen Bible study.

4 Respond

Think of a family in your congregation in which all members seem to have a strong faith. Ask your parents if you can invite them over for dinner. Ask them about their faith: What makes it so strong? What role does the church play in strengthening their faith? What things do they do together that help them grow in faith?

STRATEGIC YOUTH MINISTRY

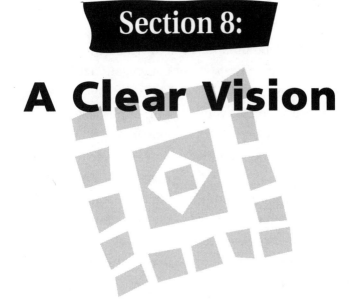

Section 8:

A Clear Vision

A Clear Vision

A clear vision and sense of purpose are essential elements of an effective youth ministry. They give you focus, direction, and energy. They help set priorities, make choices, and keep you going when the going gets tough.

Yet, too many congregations don't have a clear mission or vision statement. For example, a Search Institute study of youth workers from many denominations found that only 42 percent of congregations have a clear mission statement for their youth program.[9]

What are the keys to creating a clear vision for your congregation's youth ministry? Through its work on change in congregations, Search Institute has identified a number of key factors:

• It involves many different people in shaping and sharing the vision. It should include congregational leaders, youth, parents, other adults of all ages, youth ministry staff and volunteers, and others.

• It builds on solid, objective information about the congregation, its community, and young people in both places. This information does not have to be expensive or highly detailed, but it does need to draw from a variety of perspectives and concerns.

• It focuses on the "preferred future"—what it looks like in several years to be the kind of church that the congregation is being called to be.

The *Congregations at Crossroads* study did not ask specifically about the vision for youth ministry. But it did ask whether the congregation has a vision and whether people in the congregation could articulate the vision. Only half of all youth surveyed said their congregation has a clear vision, and only 28 percent said they could tell others what the congregation's mission or purpose is. Adults aren't much clearer; only 56 percent say their congregation has a clear vision, and only 43 percent can tell you what the congregation's purpose is. If a congregation's vision for youth grows out of a congregation-wide vision for ministry, then these findings suggest an important area of need.

Having and sharing a clear vision is not a panacea. It doesn't take away the need for hard work. Nor does it guarantee success—particularly in the short term. But you can be quite confident that a clear vision that is widely shared will become an invaluable tool for planning, setting direction, and energizing the congregation for youth ministry.

Work Sheet 9
Examining Your Congregation's Vision

Use this work sheet to think about your congregation's vision. First, rate your congregation on each of the items in the second column. Then, list in the third column things you already do to strengthen each quality. Finally, jot down other things you could do to strengthen your congregation's vision.

Qualities	Rating Your Congregation Needs Work = * OK = ** Great = ***	What We Do Now	What We Could Do Better
A clear vision for the church	___ The congregation has a clear vision of its purpose and mission.		
A clear vision for the youth ministry	___ The congregation has a clear vision for its youth ministry.		
A shared vision for the church	___ Members of the congregation, including youth, can articulate the congregation's vision and mission.		
A shared vision for the youth ministry	___ Youth and other members of the church can articulate the mission and purpose of the youth program.		

Develop a Clear Vision for Youth Ministry in the Congregation

What it is

What do you hope to accomplish in your congregation's youth ministry? In what ways do you want young people—and the world—to be different because of the energy, creativity, and commitment you put into your work with youth? Answering these kinds of questions can help set priorities and give energy to the youth ministry and congregation as a whole.

Note that the vision being suggested is a congregational vision for youth ministry. It's not the youth minister's vision or the vision of the leaders of youth ministry efforts. For a youth ministry to have lasting impact, it must become an integral part of the whole congregation's sense of vision and mission.

Talk with youth

■ What would you tell a visitor who asked you about the vision or mission of your congregation? of your youth ministry?

■ If you could name some of the most important things the youth ministry program should try to accomplish, what would they be?

■ If you don't really understand the congregation's vision or the vision for youth ministry (if it exists), what can you do to learn about it and help to shape it in the future?

Ideas to try

■ Get copies of your congregation's mission and/or vision statement(s). Rework them to reflect the dynamics of your congregation's youth ministry. Talk about what's different and what's the same.

■ Invite a cross section of the congregation (including youth, the pastor, Christian education director, parents, and others) to help create a vision for the congregation's youth ministry. Use their ideas to help guide planning and priorities.

■ Create a "dream team" of adults and youth whose task is to suggest opportunities and priorities to the leadership of the congregation.

Resources to use

M. Steven Games (editor), **Lifegivers: A Practical Guide for Reaching Youth in a Challenging World** (Abingdon Press).

Eugene C. Roehlkepartain, **Building Assets in Congregations** (Search Institute).

Doug Fields, **Purpose Driven Youth Ministry** (Zondervan).

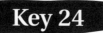

Involve Youth in Shaping and Sharing the Vision for Youth Ministry

What it is

One of the keys to developing a strong vision for a congregation and youth ministry is involving many different people in developing and sharing that vision. But too often congregations forget that young people are important voices in the process—not just for the youth ministry vision, but for the vision for the whole congregation.

In addition, young people become wonderful ambassadors for the congregation when they know and can talk about what the church is trying to accomplish. "We're a congregation that focuses on helping youth grow in their faith" sounds very different out of the mouth of a fourteen-year-old than when it is said by a forty-year-old.

Talk with youth

■ If someone asked you why you attend this congregation, what would you tell them? If they asked what makes your congregation unique, what would be your response?

■ How much do you know about the congregation's larger sense of mission and ministry? What would you most like to know?

During a youth meeting, give each person a photocopy of the "Learning Together: What's Your Congregation's Vision?" handout on page 80. Instruct youth to form groups of three and work through their handouts together.

Ideas to try

■ Whenever possible, include a short slogan based on the vision for youth ministry on newsletters, T-shirts, banners, and other visible places. Do the same with the congregation's broader vision for ministry.

■ When (not if!) you develop vision and mission statement(s) for the congregation's youth ministry, include them in the church's newsletter and bulletin. Keep the vision in front of people at all times.

■ Encourage the pastor to preach on both the congregational vision and the youth ministry vision.

Resources to use

No More Us & Them: 100 Ways to Bring Your Youth & Church Together (Group Publishing).

David Adams, et al., **An Asset Builder's Guide to Youth Leadership** (Search Institute).

Learning Together
Youth Handout

What's Your Congregation's Vision?

Try this experiment: Have someone give you a puzzle without showing or telling you anything about it—how big it is, what the picture is, and so on. Then try to put it together. It's not easy. Being in the church can be like that: It's hard to know what to do or how to contribute if you don't have the "big picture"—the vision. When you know your congregation's vision, you're more likely to actively work for that vision—and grow in your own faith in the process.

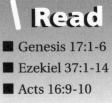
Read

■ Genesis 17:1-6
■ Ezekiel 37:1-14
■ Acts 16:9-10

Reflect

■ Each of these Bible passages describes a different type of vision. How do you think these visions guided and motivated those who first received them? How does having a "vision" for the future guide and motivate you?

■ If someone asked you what your congregation's vision is for the future, what would you say?

■ If your congregation could be known for just one thing, what would you hope it would be? With whom can you share your "vision"?

Respond

Ask your youth worker, pastor, or another leader in your congregation for a copy of the congregation's vision statement. If there isn't one, ask your pastor or youth minister to write one. Then compare that statement to what you wrote. What are the similarities and differences? Which statement do you like better? How does knowing the vision affect your feelings about the church?

React

What are the goals of your congregation? What is your congregation's reason for existing? Discuss these questions with your group, and together decide what you think your congregation's vision or mission should be. Then write that vision or mission in the space below.

_____

_____

_____

_____

_____

_____

_____

_____

Section 9:

Empowering Leadership

Empowering Leadership

Leaders in a congregation play an important role in the effectiveness of a youth program. The *Congregations at Crossroads* study—which focused on the congregation overall, not just the leadership of the youth program—found four significant influences on shaping young people's faith: the pastor, the congregation's vision, how the congregation engages people in leadership, and how the congregation deals with conflict.

Three characteristics deal with the pastor. Most youth (69 percent) see their pastor as excited about the congregation. Fewer (45 percent) report that their pastor is effective in several areas, including openness to new ideas, having the congregation's confidence, being able to motivate the congregation, and being enthusiastic.

The next set of items deal with the congregation's vision and mission. About half of the youth say their congregation has a clear vision. But only 28 percent say they can clearly explain their congregation's mission.

The way a congregation involves members, including youth, in its collective life and decisions also has an impact on young people's experience and growth. A sense of shared decision making, getting people involved, listening to each other, keeping members informed, working as a team, and using members' talents and skills are all important elements. About one-third of youth experience this kind of involvement in decision making in their congregation. Even fewer youth (19 percent) indicate that the congregation does a good job of involving youth in decision making in the congregation.

Finally, the way the congregation deals with conflict is an important factor. To some extent, every congregation will have conflict. The key is how the congregation deals with that conflict. About one-third (35 percent) of youth say their congregation does a good or excellent job of dealing with conflict openly.

Work Sheet 10
Effective Leadership

Use this work sheet to think about your congregation's leadership. First, rate your congregation on each of the items in the second column. Then, list in the third column things you already do to strengthen each quality. Finally, jot down other things you could do to strengthen your congregation's leadership.

Qualities	Rating Your Congregation Needs Work = * OK = ** Great = ***	What We Do Now	What We Could Do Better
Effective leadership	___ The pastor is open to new ideas and has the congregation's confidence. ___ The pastor is excited about the congregation and its ministry. ___ Youth program leaders are open to new ideas, have the congregation's confidence, and are excited about the youth program.		
Clear mission	___ The congregation has a clear vision of what it is trying to do. ___ Youth can explain the congregation's sense of purpose or mission. ___ The congregation has a clear vision for youth ministry.		
Lay involvement	___ Many members share responsibility for the congregation's ministry. ___ The congregation involves youth in decision making. ___ The congregation's leaders involve many people in decision making. ___ The congregation does a good job of using members' talents and skills.		

Develop an Open and Affirming Leadership Style

What it is

Leaders set a tone and direction for a congregation and its youth ministry. The *Congregations at Crossroads* study identified several dimensions of an open and affirming leadership style that contribute to a congregation's nurturing of faith. The survey focused on pastors' leadership, but these qualities are probably important for all leaders in the congregation, including youth leaders. Which of the following qualities (adapted from the survey) is true of the leadership in your congregation's ministry with youth?

___The youth leader is open to new ideas and new ways of doing things.

___Youth, parents, and other congregational members have a lot of confidence in the leadership of the youth ministry.

___The leadership of the youth ministry is good at motivating people.

___The leadership of the youth ministry is enthusiastic.

Talk with youth

■ What reactions do you get from others in the church when you share your ideas, needs, perspectives, or concerns?

■ What things make you more comfortable (or uncomfortable) with sharing your ideas with the pastor, church staff, and youth ministry leaders?

■ Who is the leader you most admire who is living today? What qualities do you most admire in that leader?

Ideas to try

■ Identify a member of the congregation who can be a leadership mentor to help you as you shape your personal leadership style.

■ Hold a retreat of church leaders, both staff and volunteers, to talk about your leadership philosophy and styles. During the retreat Bible studies and devotions, examine Jesus' leadership style.

■ Help ensure that the congregation's pastor is comfortable and open with youth by including young people on the call committee for interviewing pastoral leadership and other church staff.

Resources to use

Celia Allison Hahn, **Growing in Authority, Relinquishing Control: A New Approach to Faithful Leadership** *(Alban Institute).*

Ervin F. Henkelmann and Stephan J. Carter, **How to Develop a Team Ministry and Make It Work** *(Concordia Publishing House).*

Lovett H. Weems Jr., **Church Leadership: Vision, Team Culture, and Integrity** *(Abingdon Press).*

Michael D. Warden, **Extraordinary Results From Ordinary Teachers** *(Group Publishing).*

Foster Excitement About the Congregation and Youth Ministry Among Leaders

What it is

"Are we having fun yet?" It's a phrase that's often asked with a hint of irony or sarcasm. But without the "fun factor," life can get dull and boring. The result is drained energy, dwindling creativity, and many excuses for not getting involved. Enthusiasm and excitement are hard to measure, but you know when they're present. They're like the leavening that gives bread its life and texture. (You can eat bread without yeast, but it tends to be a lot more work!) Enthusiasm builds energy and commitment; apathy drains them away.

The national study focused on the pastor's enthusiasm. But it's also important that all leaders and participants share that enthusiasm. Paying attention to the energy level and fun factor in your planning and your events can make all the difference in the effectiveness of your ministries.

Talk with youth

■ What's the most exciting event you've participated in at church? What made it exciting to you?

■ What does the congregation get excited about? What do youth get excited about in the church?

■ What happens in the congregation that drains your energy and enthusiasm? What adds energy and commitment? What can we do to decrease the "energy drainers" and increase the "energy adders"?

Ideas to try

■ Each year (or more often), celebrate accomplishments in fulfilling the congregation's mission and ministry with an all-church party.

■ Invite congregational leaders to youth events to get them more interested and involved.

■ Have youth write a column in the church newsletter that reports on the exciting things that are happening among youth in the congregation.

■ Encourage the practice of a sabbatical leave at least every seven years for staff and volunteers in youth ministry so they get revitalized for continuing service.

Resources to use

Robert D. Dale, **Keeping the Dream Alive** *(Broadman Press).*

Lyle E. Schaller, **Activating the Passive Church: Diagnosis and Treatment** *(Abingdon Press).*

Involve Youth in Congregational Decision Making

What it is

Youth can play a role in making decisions both for youth ministry programs and activities as well as decisions regarding the congregation as a whole. Evaluate how well your congregation involves youth in decision making using the following statements, which are adapted from the national study to focus on youth. How many of these items are true for your congregation?

___Leaders like to involve many youth in making important decisions about youth ministry as well as the larger congregation.

___Youth have a lot of say when important decisions are made in the congregation.

___Adults listen to each other and to youth.

___Leaders keep youth informed about important issues in the congregation.

___Youth and adults are good at working together as a team.

- -

Talk with youth

■ How often do you feel your ideas and input are sought for planning youth ministry? for planning other ministries in the congregation?

■ In what areas do you feel you have a say in the congregation's decision making? In what areas do you feel you have no say?

■ What would make you feel more comfortable to be a part of congregational decision making (for example, skills, affirmation, or acceptance)?

During a youth meeting, give each person a photocopy of the "Learning Together: Finding Your Place" handout on page 87. Instruct youth to form groups of three and complete their handouts in their groups.

Ideas to try

■ Have young people be the primary decision makers in shaping the congregation's youth program. Be sure to train and support them so they can be effective in this role.

■ Take time in youth group settings to talk about issues, needs, programs, and emphases in the congregation and youth ministry. Connect it to the specific areas they can be involved.

■ Talk with congregational leaders about how to make decision-making processes more interesting and relevant to youth. Take time to educate youth about how the congregation operates and why.

■ Have youth elect representatives to serve on the congregation's council as at-large members. Or form a youth advisory council to recommend to the council specific actions for staffing, building, programs, and other areas of ministry.

Resources to use

Thom and Joani Schultz, **Kids Taking Charge: Youth-Led Youth Ministry** *(Group Publishing).*

Ray Johnston, **Developing Student Leaders** *(Youth Specialties).*

Training Youth for Dynamic Leadership *(Group Publishing).*

David Adams et al., **An Asset Builder's Guide to Youth Leadership** *(Search Institute).*

Learning Together
Youth Handout

Finding Your Place

It was like a ritual. Every Sunday night John, Jean, Phil, and Denise would go out for a hamburger or pizza after youth group. And each week, they'd complain about someone or something at church. Maybe the walls at church were painted a weird color, or the congregation didn't like up-beat hymns, or the mission trips were never scheduled at a good time. Of course, John, Jean, Phil, and Denise might be able to address some of these issues if they joined the youth council or volunteered for a committee. But then what would they talk about on Sunday nights?

1 Read

- Exodus 4:11-17
- Acts 6:2-7
- 1 Timothy 4:11-16

2 Reflect

- Being involved in church decisions is an important task with important responsibilities. What do these passages say about the responsibilities of decision makers—of any age?
- What unique perspectives do you and other people your age bring to decisions your congregation needs to make?
- What kinds of decision-making roles do you already play in your congregation and elsewhere? What other kinds of decision making would you like to be involved in your congregation?

4 Respond

Get permission to attend a meeting of your congregation's board or another committee that interests you. You may want to attend with a partner or a group of people. Find out how decisions are made and ways you might be able to participate in decision making. Talk with your parents and youth workers about roles that might be appropriate for you.

3 React

Who are the decision makers in your congregation? Are they adults? Are they young people? Is your pastor the person who makes most of the decisions? Are there volunteer leaders who are involved?

There are many qualities and skills people have that make them good at making decisions. Some are very quiet and listen a lot so they know what other people want and can base their decisions on that. Others gather a lot of information so they can make well-informed decisions. Still others know how to lead good conversations and get a group of people to agree to a common decision.

Talk with your group about who you think are some of the decision makers in your church. On the page below, list three decision makers in your church. Next to each name, write qualities you think help make that person good at making decisions (for example: Marion White—good listener, knows a lot of people in the congregation).

Name: _____

Qualities: _____

Name: _____

Qualities: _____

Name: _____

Qualities: _____

Foster in Youth a Sense of Responsibility for the Congregation's Ministry

What it is

Congregations often include a list of staff on the back of their worship bulletins and newsletters. From time to time, you'll see one that reads, "Ministers: the 200 members. Pastor: Rev. Clarence Johnston."

These congregations aren't just trying to get people's attention. They're reminding people that the real work of the church is the job of the members. It's not the pastor's job to do all the caring, serving, teaching, evangelizing. Those are the tasks to which all Christians have been called. The pastor's job is to "equip the saints" for these ministries. The Search Institute study of LCMS youth and adults found that one key to nurturing faith in a congregation is having members feel a sense of shared responsibility for the congregation's ministries. However, only 36 percent of youth feel such responsibility. Not only is shared ministry the most effective way to accomplish the mission of the church, it's also an essential way to nurture in young people a sense of living out their own calling as part of the body of Christ.

Resources to use

Oscar Feucht, **Everyone a Minister** *(Concordia Publishing House).*

Core Belief Bible Study Series: Why the Church Matters *(Group Publishing).*

Core Belief Bible Study Series: The Truth About the Church *(Group Publishing).*

Talk with youth

■ In which congregational ministries do you feel a sense of responsibility? In which do you feel left out of? Which ones would you like to contribute to?

■ If you were running the congregation, which ministries would you emphasize? stop? start?

Ideas to try

■ Invite youth to plan and participate in a variety of congregational ministries beyond the youth program, including Sunday school for younger children, vacation Bible school, programs for special groups such as the elderly or disabled, congregation-wide service projects, and special task forces.

■ Include youth in regular roles in the congregation as you would with adults, including participation on boards and committees, volunteering for "kitchen duty" or church cleanup days, and other tasks.

■ Be sure young people are included in the congregation's stewardship campaigns and pledging. Encourage them to give to the congregational ministries just as you encourage adults to give.

■ Invite pastors and other staff members to meet with young people three or four times each year to gather ideas and opinions on the congregation's ministries.

Key 29

Use Young People's Talents in the Congregation

What it is

A youth worker in Florida was frustrated. He wanted to tap the talents of his youth group, but couldn't figure out anything the kids had in common. Some liked acting, while others couldn't stand being in front of people. Some liked art, while others were great at working with younger children. So he got together with the group, and they brainstormed. What they came up with was a youth-led clown ministry that allowed the actors to act, the artists to do art, the people who work with children to interact with children, and so forth. Everyone found a way to contribute. And the ministry gave a message of hope and good cheer in nursing homes, at hospitals, in the community, as well as in the congregation. Sometimes we think of talents in narrow ways (usually music or some other "up-front" gift). But every young person in the congregation has something to contribute. We just have to take time to get to know them and then find ways to connect their gifts with the ministry of the congregation.

Talk with youth

■ In what areas of your life do you feel that your talents are most valued, such as in your family, school, community, and church? What happens in these places that make you feel valued?

■ What kinds of talents and gifts seem to be most valued in the congregation? How can we "make room" for other talents as well?

■ If you could give just one gift or talent to the congregation, what would you give? Why?

Ideas to try

■ Have a Bible study with youth that focuses on spiritual gifts and talents.

■ Ask youth to identify their own talents and then brainstorm about ways they could use those talents in the church (even if there are not any current "slots" for volunteers with their particular interests).

■ Appoint a young person to be a "talent scout" for the congregation. He or she can watch for hidden talents and interests among youth and then encourage youth to share these gifts with the congregation.

■ Match youth with adults who have similar interests and talents such as music, banner-making, property maintenance, expressing care for others, and writing. Have them work together to contribute to the church while also nurturing the young person's talents and relationships.

Resources to use

Brian Kelley Bauknight, **Body Building: Creating a Ministry Team Through Spiritual Gifts** *(Abingdon Press)*.

Sue Mallory, Sara Jane Rhenborg, and Brad Smith, **The Starter Kit for Mobilizing Ministry** *(Leadership Network)*.

Training Youth for Dynamic Leadership *(Group Publishing)*.

Be Open to New Ideas to Strengthen the Congregation and Youth Ministry

What it is

A bout two out of five LCMS youth say their congregation "is ready and willing to change when a good new idea comes along." But you don't have to wait passively for new ideas to come along. You can go looking for them. Try the following:

• Visit other up-and-coming congregations to see what they're doing that makes a difference—even if you disagree with their theology.

• Attend youth ministry conferences and workshops, particularly if you have opportunities to attend local events sponsored by other Christian denominations and organizations.

• Regularly visit places where kids spend time, such as schools, community youth programs, zoos, malls, and parks.

• Read magazines and newsletters from other disciplines that serve youth, especially some of the many magazines for public school teachers.

Talk with youth

■ What's your perception of change in the congregation? Does it take forever to change anything? Or do things happen so fast that you always feel a little disoriented?

■ If you could change one thing about this congregation, what would it be? Why?

■ What's the most creative thing that has happened in this congregation? What made it successful (or interfered with its success)?

During a youth meeting, give each person a photocopy of the "Learning Together: A Change Can Do You Good" handout on page 91. Instruct youth to find partners and complete the handout in pairs.

Ideas to try

■ Pretend you're starting a brand-new youth ministry in a brand-new church that has ample resources. What would the youth program look like? Now, what are some ways you could introduce elements of this innovative ministry into your own congregation?

■ Start a "Top That Idea" letter among your friends in youth ministry (either in the congregation or from multiple congregations). Send a program idea to the first person, who then tries to make the program more innovative and sends the letter to the next person. Continue until the idea gets back to the first person.

Resources to use

Loren B. Mead, **The Once and Future Church: Reinventing the Congregation for a New Mission Frontier** *(Alban Institute).*

C. Jeff Woods, **We've Never Done It Like This Before: Ten Creative Approaches to the Same Old Church Tasks** *(Alban Institute).*

Leonard Sweet, **AquaChurch: Essential Leadership Arts for Piloting Your Church in Today's Fluid Culture** *(Group Publishing).*

Learning Together
Youth Handout

A Change Can Do You Good

Some people like change just for the sake of changing. That's probably not a very good reason to make many changes. But changes that are well thought out can bring many good things to congregations:

- Creative ideas and solutions
- Hope for a better congregation and community
- Advances in the congregation's mission
- New opportunities and friendships
- Growth in commitment
- Energy, enthusiasm, and excitement

❚ Read

■ Exodus 17:1-7
■ Job 1:13-22
■ Luke 24:36-53

2 Reflect

■ Each of these Bible stories talks about people facing change. What did they do to deal with change that can help you better work through changes in your own life?

■ What are some examples of change that have happened in your congregation? What has been exciting about those changes? What has been hard?

■ What kinds of changes are hard to deal with in your congregation? Why?

3 React

Think of a time in your life when you faced a major change. Describe the change to your partner and why it had to be made. Then answer these questions:

- Was preparing for that change scary? exciting? sad? Explain.
- How did you feel after you made the change?
- Why do you think change is sometimes difficult?

4 Respond

Think about one specific change you think would be good for your congregation. List all the people and groups in the congregation who would be affected by the change and how they might respond. Talk with others in your congregation about what would need to happen for that change to take place. See if you can start the change process.

_____

_____

_____

_____

Section 10:

Focusing Your Youth Ministry Four Planning Sessions

Faith Maturity– A Focus for Youth Ministry

Session Purpose

To help youth and their leaders understand the dimensions of faith maturity and how this framework provides a lens for assessing, reflecting on, and planning a focused youth ministry.

Getting Started

Welcome participants as they arrive. Explain the purpose of the session and the three sessions that follow: To focus on how the congregation nurtures faith in youth and to plan for the future. Stress the importance of people attending all four sessions (or as many as you will be offering). Then open with prayer or a devotional of your choice.

Portraits of Faith

Form small teams of three or four. (If your group is inter-generational, be sure to include people from different generations in each group.) Give each team a sheet of newsprint and an assortment of colorful markers.

SAY: I'd like each group to draw a portrait of a young person with a deep and strong faith. Use symbols, stick figures, or whatever other techniques you'd like. When you're finished, you'll have a chance to share your picture with the others who are here today.

Give groups five to ten minutes to complete their assignments. Then ask a spokesperson from each team to describe its portrait and post it on a wall. After all the teams have shared, point out common features and

What You'll Need

For the leader and group activities:

- several sheets of newsprint
- bold, nontoxic markers
- a copy of Work Sheet 11 (p. 97), cut into strips
- a poster or sheet of newsprint that lists the nine indicators of faith maturity from Work Sheet 11

For each participant:

- a pen or pencil
- colorful, nontoxic markers
- a copy of Work Sheet 12 (p. 98) and Work Sheet 13 (p. 99)

Optional (for alternative closings):

- a soft ball, stuffed animal, or other soft object to toss; or
- a candle and matches

differences among the posters.

THEN SAY: In reality, it's impossible to draw a picture of what faith looks like, since faith is a gift from God, not something we earn or do. But many of the things we've included in our portraits of young people are the signs that people express when their faith is strong and growing.

Search Institute has developed a framework called "faith maturity" to give a glimpse of how Christians express their faith. This framework helps us think about the central purpose of youth ministry in our congregation: helping young people grow and mature in faith.

In this session, we'll use the faith maturity framework to reflect on our own faith and how this congregation can and does help youth grow in faith. In the sessions that follow, we'll continue our planning by looking at qualities of congregations that research has shown to be important in nurturing a mature faith.

Faith Maturity

Give each team one or more of the indicator strips from Work Sheet 11, "Nine Indicators of Faith

Maturity." **SAY:** Search Institute has identified nine indicators of faith maturity. Each of the strips I gave you represents one of these indicators. The indicators are not "tests" of faith, but helpful ways for us to think about how we live and express our faith day by day.

Have teams rotate among the posters created earlier and mark things on the posters that are described on the indicator of faith. For example, the team with the "seeks spiritual growth" strip might circle a Bible in the person's hand to highlight reading the Bible as a way of growing spiritually. If a team cannot find anything on a particular poster that fits the indicator, have team members brainstorm about what they could add and then add it.

When all the teams have analyzed all the posters, have each team describe to the whole group its indicator of faith maturity and some of the symbols it found on the portraits that fit with that indicator. (It's OK if several groups chose the same symbols.) Ask:

• Which indicators were easiest to find symbols for? hardest? Why?

• How did our experience in this activity reflect our own priorities and our congregation's emphases? How was it different?

• What questions do these indicators of faith raise for you?

• In what ways do these indicators challenge us to think about new things?

Reflecting on Experiences

Display your poster listing the nine indicators of faith maturity (see "What You'll Need"). **SAY:** These indicators of faith maturity are not just an intellectual exercise. They can touch our lives deeply and personally as individuals and as a congregation. I'd like us to spend some time reflecting on our experiences of faith maturity in our own lives and in our congregation.

Give each person a copy of Work Sheet 12 (p. 98). **SAY:** As we think about our own faith and how faith is expressed in our congregation, it's important to be honest about where we are on this journey and what

we need to keep us traveling on the path of discipleship and growth. It's on the basis of our strengths and needs and our understanding of what God is saying to us through our situation that we can plan for more effective youth ministry.

Let's begin with our own lives. When you think about your own experience of faith, what are you pleased about? What troubles you?

Give an example or two from your own life. For instance, you may be pleased about your participation in service projects (Acts and Serves), but troubled that your prayer life is inconsistent (Seeks Spiritual Growth). Ask participants to jot on their work sheets a few words about their own experiences. Give them two to four minutes.

SAY: You'll not be asked to share this information. Write in code if you wish. This is for your personal use only, to help each of us think about our own experience, not just the experience of "people out there."

Now think of other youth in our congregation. When you think of how they express their faith in their lives, what are you pleased about? What bothers you? Jot down a few words on the work sheet. Take a couple of minutes for this, also. You will not be asked to hand in this work sheet. Your jottings are simply to help jog your memory for our conversation in a few minutes.

Have participants form small groups of three or four people each. Try to have adults and youth in each group. Within each group, ask participants to take turns telling one thing that pleases him or her very much about the faith life of youth in the congregation. When everyone has shared, have members each share in their groups things that trouble them. Allow about ten minutes.

Using a bold marker, make two columns on a sheet of newsprint: "Pleased" and "Troubled." Ask for "Pleased" responses from all of the groups. Jot key words in the "Pleased" column. Then ask for "Troubled" responses, and jot those down. Invite participants to help identify the most significant themes in both columns.

Next Steps and Closing

Decide what to do next and who will do what to prepare for future planning sessions. Use Work Sheet 13 (p. 99) as a guide for tracking your next steps.

Ask participants each to name the discovery or insight from the session that was most important to them. You may want to go around more than once to give each group member a chance to mention more than one idea. Write each discovery on newsprint. Save these newsprint pages for use in later planning sessions.

Close with a prayer or song chosen by the youth.

Alternative Closings

• Have people toss a ball, stuffed animal, or other soft object from one person to the next as they name a discovery or insight from the session. (This activity may be especially helpful if the youth are getting restless or if some people have been shy or otherwise reluctant to participate.)

• Create a more subdued, reflective closing by lighting a candle and having it passed around as each participant names a discovery or insight.

Work Sheet 11
Nine Indicators of Faith Maturity

Copy this page and cut apart the strips to use in the group activity.

Indicator 1: Trusts and Believes—Trusting in God's saving grace and believing firmly in Jesus Christ's humanity and divinity.

Indicator 2: Experiences the Fruits of Faith—Experiencing a sense of well-being, security, and peace in one's life.

Indicator 3: Integrates Faith and Life—Integrating faith and life, seeing work, family, political choices, and social relationships as part of one's religious life.

Indicator 4: Celebrates the Good News—Celebrating the good news of God's work in individuals' lives.

Indicator 5: Seeks Spiritual Growth—Seeking spiritual growth through study, reflection, prayer, and discussion with others.

Indicator 6: Nurtures Faith in Community—Seeking to be part of a community of believers in which people give witness to their faith and support one another.

Indicator 7: Holds Life-Affirming Values—Holding life-affirming values, including a commitment to the equality of all people, an affirmation of cultural and religious diversity, and a personal sense of responsibility for the welfare of others.

Indicator 8: Advocates Social Change—Advocating social change to improve human welfare.

Indicator 9: Acts and Serves—Serving humanity consistently and passionately through acts of love and compassion.

Work Sheet 12

The Shape of Faith in Our Own Lives and in Our Congregation

1. On the chart below, take a moment to jot down a few key words about your own experience of growing in faith maturity. (Keep in mind all nine indicators of faith maturity.) What are you pleased about? troubled about? You will not be asked to share this information. Write in code if you wish.

2. What about other youth in your congregation? Jot a couple of "Pleased" and "Troubled" notes in the "Other Youth in Our Congregation" boxes.

	Pleased	**Troubled**
Myself		
Other Youth in Our Congregation		

Work Sheet 13
Our Team's Next Steps

When our team will meet again: _____

Who else we'd like to have meet with us:

_____

_____

_____

_____

Who will be in charge of guiding our next conversation:

_____

_____

_____

_____

Things we need to do to follow up from this session:

_____

_____

_____

_____

Things to bring up again for discussion:

_____

_____

_____

_____

Other things we need to talk about:

_____

_____

_____

_____

_____

Qualities of Faith-Nurturing Congregations

Session Purpose

To help youth and adults reflect on the shape of youth ministry in their congregation in light of the thirty-four qualities of faith-nurturing congregations identified in national research.

Getting Started

Welcome everyone to this second session. Post the newsprint sheets from session 1. Review the discussion from the first session, using the newsprint sheets you posted to refresh people's memory. Take time to listen to any thoughts people had about young people's experiences in your congregation since you were last together.

Read a Scripture passage that focuses on the congregation as the body of Christ working together in mutual support and appreciation (such as 1 Thessalonians 5:14-18). Follow the Scripture reading with prayer. For the prayer, consider inviting each person to mention something he or she is grateful for in your congregation.

What You'll Need

For the leader and group activities:

- a Bible
- eight sheets of newsprint, each labeled with one category of the qualities of faith-nurturing congregations (see Work Sheet 14 on page 103)
- easel and additional newsprint
- bold, nontoxic markers
- masking tape
- a ball of yarn or string
- newsprint sheets from session 1
- a balloon or beach ball (optional)

For each participant:

- a pen or pencil
- a copy of Work Sheet 14 (p. 103), Work Sheet 15 (pp. 104-105), and Work Sheet 16 (p. 106)
- three green dots (self-adhesive labels) and three orange dots (If you don't have dots, give each person two colors of markers.)

start, since nurturing faith is probably the most important goal in our youth ministry.

Today we're going to look at how our congregation can and does nurture faith. We're going to do this using an approach based on Search Institute research that identified qualities in congregational life that directly impact people's faith maturity. In a major study of youth and adults, Search Institute identified thirty-four qualities of congregations that, when present, help youth have a stronger faith. (Note: The study identified thirty qualities important for nurturing adults' faith.) **The more of these qualities that are present in a congregation, the more likely youth are to have a faith that's lived out in action and devotion in daily life.**

Distribute the fact sheet titled "Qualities of Faith-Nurturing Congregations—Summary" (Work Sheet 14, p. 103). Explain that the qualities of faith-nurturing congregations can be grouped into the eight listed categories. Once everyone has grasped the big picture, then you'll look at the thirty-four specific qualities that fit in these eight categories.

Understanding the Qualities of Faith-Nurturing Congregations

SAY: In our first session, we focused on the shape of faith maturity in our lives and the lives of young people in our congregation. This was an important place to

Briefly discuss each of the eight categories. Note that the categories extend beyond the formal youth program to include the many different ways the whole congregation influences young people's faith.

Form four small groups, and assign each group two of the categories to discuss. (If your group has more than thirty participants, form eight groups, assigning each group one category.) After everyone has introduced herself or himself, ask each person to share with the small group the following:

• **Tell about a time you have experienced or seen some aspect of this category in this or another congregation.**

• **How has this category had an impact on your own faith or the faith of others?**

Give groups five to seven minutes to discuss. Then ask each small group to describe their category and report two or three highlights or themes from their discussion.

Assessing the Qualities in Our Congregation

Distribute to each person Work Sheet 15, "Qualities of Faith-Nurturing Congregations—Checklist" (pp. 104-105). Explain that this sheet fills in the eight categories you've just discussed with specific qualities. Note the overlap between some of the individual qualities and the discussion of people's experiences in the congregation.

Give people time to complete the checklist individually. While they're working, post around the room the newsprint sheets you created for the eight categories (see "What You'll Need"). Then give each person three green dots and three orange dots. (If you don't have dots, give each participant—or have them share—two colors of markers or have them mark "x" or "o" with a single marker.)

Point out the eight categories that you have posted around the room. Have people add their dots to the signs as follows:

• a green dot on each of the three categories they feel most glad about in their congregation, and

• an orange dot on each of the three categories they feel most sad about in their congregation.

When all the dots have been placed, invite participants to note patterns in their voting. How do they interpret those patterns? Ask about whether there are differences between the youth program itself and the general culture of the congregation regarding these qualities.

Note the group's comments on the sheets of newsprint. Save the dotted category sheets for use in session 3.

Creating a Web

SAY: Sometimes when we talk about priorities and things to do, we get overwhelmed or assume that someone else is responsible for making things happen. While the kinds of things we've talked about do require a lot of time and energy from many people, each of us can do things—right away—that can make a difference. The choices we make, the things we spend time doing, our own priorities can all help make some of these things happen.

Give an example based on the priorities the group identified. For instance, if creating a more engaging climate was a priority, mention ways people can, on their own, help the congregation have a more engaging climate. That might include being conscious about greeting people they don't know or taking time to have at least one good conversation with someone at church each week.

THEN SAY: At the same time, a congregation needs all its parts working together to nurture faith and to strengthen the qualities we've identified. It takes all the members working together to create the web of qualities that make up a faith-nurturing congregation.

Ask everyone to look again at the checklist of qualities of faith-nurturing congregations and pick out two that they especially value to keep in mind for this exercise. Then form a circle.

SAY: We're going to create a web of these qualities to symbolize how they support young people growing up in their faith. I'll begin by naming a quality. I'll hold on to the end of the yarn and toss the ball of yarn to someone across the circle. That person will catch the yarn, name a quality that he or she values, and toss the ball to someone else while holding on to the yarn. We'll continue until everyone has had an opportunity to name two qualities that they particularly value.

This activity takes just a few minutes and creates a lot of laughter and fun. If some people have trouble remembering a quality to mention, others can offer to help them out with suggestions. People can repeat qualities others mentioned.

When the web is complete, you may want to toss a balloon or beach ball on top of the web, symbolizing how all the named qualities support young people in their growth in faith. Then you can carefully lower the web to the floor, tape it in place, and keep it (for a while) as a strong visual reminder to everyone of the key insights of the session.

Next Steps and Closing

Before you close, decide what to do next and who will do what in preparation for any future meetings on this session's topic. Use the "Our Team's Next Steps" handout (Work Sheet 16, p. 106) for this process.

Close with a prayer or song chosen by the youth.

Work Sheet 14

Qualities of Faith-Nurturing Congregations–Summary

1. Engaging Climate

When a congregation is warm, intellectually engaging, energized, and free of conflict, people's faith life is more likely to thrive. A climate in which youth are encouraged and expected to learn and think and ask questions about their faith helps them grow in their faith.

2. Caring Community

Beyond giving a warm welcome, members in a caring congregation take time to get to know each other. They can count on others in the congregation to help them with their personal needs. Caring goes beyond the congregation as members extend their love and concern to people in the community.

3. Effective Christian Education

Effective Christian education for all ages is essential for a faith-nurturing congregation. Learning processes that engage people in interaction with the leader and with each other (interactive learning) have a significant impact on faith.

4. Evangelism and Mission Emphasis

The Great Commission calls Christians to "go and make disciples of all nations" (Matthew 28:19). Yet few adults or youth report strength in this area in their congregations. It's interesting to note that thirteen- to fourteen-year-olds are the most likely of all age groups (including adults) to say their congregations effectively teach them to share their faith.

5. Inspiring Worship for Youth

Among adults, four out of five rate their worship experiences highly. A different picture emerges for youth. Just over half of youth report experiencing inspiring worship. Furthermore, they are much less likely to say that their congregation has strong preaching (youth: 50 percent; adults: 78 percent).

6. Support for Families

Only one in five adults who have children reported receiving help from the congregation in nurturing the faith of their children. Particularly noteworthy is that twenty- to twenty-nine-year-olds are the least likely of all parents to say they receive help from their congregation in nurturing their children's faith.

7. A Clear Vision

Only 29 percent of youth surveyed can articulate their congregation's vision. When members can tell you the congregation's vision for its work, the congregation is more likely to be effective in nurturing a dynamic faith.

8. Empowering Leadership

People whose congregations engage many people in leadership and service are more likely to be growing in their faith. Congregations that tend to deal well with conflict create an environment in which people are more likely to grow. Involving youth in congregational decision making has an impact on the faith development of young people.

Work Sheet 15

Qualities of Faith-Nurturing Congregations–Checklist

Use this checklist to assess these qualities in your own congregation. Check mark the qualities that you think most young people experience in your congregation.

Qualities	**Your Church**
Engaging Climate	
1. The congregation has a warm, welcoming, and friendly climate.	❑
2. The congregation has a thinking climate that encourages questions and expects learning.	❑
3. The congregation experiences little conflict.	❑
4. People are excited about the congregation and its ministry.	❑
5. Adults and children spend quality time together.	❑
Caring Community	
6. The congregation helps members meet their personal needs.	❑
7. People feel that others in the congregation care about them.	❑
8. People take time to get to know each other.	❑
9. The congregation shows love and concern for people in the community.	❑
10. Youth often experience care and support from an adult.	❑
Effective Christian Education	
11. The congregation has quality youth education.	❑
12. The congregation has quality adult education.	❑
13. People spend three or more hours per month in Christian education.	❑
14. Christian education for all ages emphasizes interactive learning.	❑
15. The congregation offers excellent Bible study.	❑
16. The congregation makes Scripture come alive for all ages.	❑
17. The congregation helps members apply faith to daily life.	❑
18. The congregation has quality education for children.	❑

Qualities	Your Church

Evangelism and Mission Emphasis

19. The congregation emphasizes evangelism and missions. ❑

20. The congregation teaches people how to share their faith with others. ❑

Inspiring Worship for Youth

21. The congregation has strong preaching. ❑

22. People get a lot out of worship. ❑

Support for Families

23. The congregation intentionally strengthens family life. ❑

24. The congregation helps parents learn how to nurture the faith of their children. ❑

A Clear Vision

25. The congregation has a clear vision. ❑

26. Members can explain their congregation's vision. ❑

Empowering Leadership

27. The congregation's leaders are open and affirming. ❑

28. The congregation's leaders are excited about the congregation. ❑

29. The congregation involves many people in decision making. ❑

30. Many members share responsibility for the congregation's ministry. ❑

31. The congregation makes use of members' talents. ❑

32. The congregation is open to change. ❑

33. The congregation deals well with conflict. ❑

34. The congregation involves youth in decision making. ❑

Work Sheet 16
Our Team's Next Steps

When our team will meet again: _____

Who else we'd like to have meet with us:

_____

_____

_____

_____

Who will be in charge of guiding our next conversation:

_____

_____

_____

_____

Things we need to do to follow up from this session:

_____

_____

_____

_____

Things to bring up again for discussion:

_____

_____

_____

_____

Other things we need to talk about:

_____

_____

_____

_____

_____

_____

Creating Priorities and Pictures of the Future

Session Purpose

To guide participants to identify one or two key changes they want to make in youth ministry over the next two or three years and to create a picture in their minds of the future they prefer in one area.

Getting Started

Welcome everyone to this third planning session. Ask people to share any insights or thoughts they have had about this planning process since the second session. Remind participants what you did in the first two sessions:

• Session 1 focused on faith maturity among youth in the congregation. (Mention one or two highlights from that discussion.)

• Session 2 focused on qualities of the congregation that help nurture growth in faith. (Mention one or two highlights from that discussion.)

Have everyone form a large circle. **SAY:** *To begin our session today, I'd like the discussion from last time to be the basis for our prayer together, thanking God for the areas of strength and asking for clarity and insight in addressing areas for growth and change.*

One by one, place in the center of the circle the posters of the eight categories (with dots on them) that were created in the second session. As you lay down each one, invite one or two participants to voice sentence prayers of thanksgiving or petition regarding that area of your congregation's life. For example, someone might offer thanks for all the warm relationships among youth when you place down the "Engaging Climate"

What You'll Need

For the leader and group activities:

■ eight posters with dots (from session 2)

■ newsprint and easel

■ bold, nontoxic markers

■ masking tape

■ craft supplies such as paper, newsprint, markers, art supplies, building blocks, chenille wires, and modeling clay

For each participant:

■ two sticky notes

■ a pen or pencil

■ cookies (preferably homemade)

■ a copy of Work Sheet 17 (p. 110)

poster. Go through all eight categories. Conclude the prayer time by asking for clarity and insight in choosing areas to focus on for planning.

If You Ran the Youth Ministry

Post the eight posters representing the eight categories of faith-nurturing qualities on walls around the room. If needed, give people additional time to ask questions and reflect on the discussion during (and since) the two previous sessions. Some people may want to comment on patterns they've seen and new insights they've had since you were last together.

THEN SAY: In every congregation, there are dozens of things that could be done to strengthen youth ministry. It's easy to get overwhelmed with all the possibilities and—as a result—end up not doing anything.

In this session, we'll identify one or two areas that we believe the congregation—including us—needs to make top priority in youth ministry for the next two or three years. This isn't to say that other concerns aren't important or even essential. But it does say, "This is what we can do right now." In the future, we may be able to come back and tackle another area as well.

Give each person two sticky notes and a pen or pencil. **SAY:** Let's suppose, for a moment, that you ran the youth ministry in your congregation. The church has promised to provide everything you need to make the congregation a more faith-nurturing community for youth. What would be the two most important concerns you'd want to address? (You don't need to know how you'd address them, just that they would be priorities.) Write one priority concern on each note. For example, one concern might be that young people aren't active leaders in the youth program.

Have people stick each of their completed notes on or near the posters that they think best matches their ideas. For example, the concern about youth not being active leaders would go on the "Empowering Leadership" poster. When everyone has finished, read through the notes one category at a time, particularly remarking on any areas where several people said the same thing. Group similar notes together on the wall.

Based on the number of sticky notes on each of the eight categories, work with the whole group to come to a consensus of the two concerns that they believe must be top priorities. Mention that you'll keep track of all of the ideas as the congregation continues to plan youth ministry. (If your group is large, don't try to come to a consensus; simply pick the two or three areas where most of the ideas cluster.)

SAY: It will take quite a bit of time to explore both of these priorities in any depth. For this planning session, we need to focus on just one concern so we can learn together how to work through a change. Later we can go back and work through a similar planning process for the other priority.

Have participants vote on which of the two priorities to focus on for the remainder of the session. If there is a lot of disagreement, choose one priority and promise to plan another similar session soon to address the other concern.

Creating Pictures of a Preferred Future

SAY: Sometimes when we plan, we jump right away into problem solving. So, for example, if hardly anyone shows up for service projects, we brainstorm lots of different ways to entice more people to get involved. Sometimes solving problems is exactly what we need to do. But long-term planning is much more effective when it's based, not on solving problems, but on a vision or a preferred picture of the future.

Form small groups of three to five people (a mixture of youth and adults). **SAY:** Imagine it's three years from now, and the priority concern we've identified has been addressed and the change is now a reality. As a group, brainstorm about what the change looks like in action. What's happening in the congregation? Who's doing what? with whom? Where are they? How do they feel?

For example:

• If their priority concern is that youth who aren't already in the youth group don't feel welcome, create a picture of what the youth group would look like if everyone did feel welcome.

• If their priority concern is that youth and adults are very separated from each other in all the programs of the church, and they want them to be more closely connected, create a picture of what youth and adults being together would look like.

• If their priority for change is that worship is dull for youth, ask them to create a picture of a worship service that tells what they want it to be like.

Then encourage small groups to have fun working together creating an image, symbol, or picture of the way they want things to be in that area three years from now. Provide paper, newsprint, markers, art supplies, building blocks, chenille wires, modeling clay, and other materials that might be useful. (Some groups might prefer to prepare a skit or other type of presentation.) Give the small groups ten to fifteen minutes to create their image.

Then have each group present its creation to the whole group, explaining the meaning behind their image of the future. Encourage other participants to respond by mentioning other meanings they saw in the creations—perhaps even meanings the creators didn't originally intend.

Listen for themes running through the presentations and jot them on newsprint as the groups share. Then have the whole group work together to combine those main ideas into one or two sentences about what they want to see in your youth ministry in the future. Write these sentences on a fresh sheet of newsprint labeled "Our Picture of the Future." Try to achieve a consensus, with everyone feeling comfortable about the statement. Save this sheet for use in session 4.

SAY: What we've done, essentially, is to create a vision for our congregation's youth ministry in one priority area of concern. This vision can help guide and motivate us as we do the practical work of planning and putting things in place that help us make a change happen. Next time we'll focus on what we can do to begin bringing this vision closer to reality.

Next Steps and Closing

Decide what to do next and who will do what in preparation for any future meetings on this session's topic. Use Work Sheet 17 for this process.

To begin the closing, pass around a plate of cookies (preferably homemade), and invite each person to take one but not eat it yet. **SAY:** It's easy to take cookies for granted. But cookies don't just suddenly appear. Someone has to decide that they want to make cookies. Then they gather and prepare the ingredients (some may already be in the cupboard, while others might need to be purchased). They mix everything together, prepare the dough, then let the cookies bake. None of those activities happens unless someone gets an idea that they want or need some cookies!

Note parallels between the cookies and the vision-based planning process. For example:

• Deciding that something is a priority is not enough. You have to follow through by "gathering the ingredients" to make change occur.

• Many of the "ingredients" for your youth ministry

vision are probably already available in your congregation.

• Even when you've done a lot of planning and work, it takes time for changes to "bake." Sometimes waiting for changes to occur is the hardest part of the whole process.

Offer a prayer of thanksgiving for the guidance that God is giving in this process and a request for the help needed to make the preferred future become real.

THEN SAY: Fortunately, it doesn't take as long to prepare cookies as it takes for major changes to become firmly planted in our congregation. The cookies are ready now, so let's enjoy them!

Work Sheet 17
Our Team's Next Steps

When our team will meet again: _____

_____

_____

_____

Who else we'd like to have meet with us: _____

_____

_____

_____

Who will be in charge of guiding our next conversation: _____

_____

_____

_____

Things we need to do to follow up from this session: _____

_____

_____

_____

Things to bring up again for discussion: _____

_____

_____

_____

Other things we need to talk about: _____

_____

_____

_____

STRATEGIC YOUTH MINISTRY

Building Support and Taking Steps

Session Purpose

To help youth and their leaders to begin creating an action plan to gain support and involvement from others in the congregation for the "picture of the future" and to begin implementing activities that will help move them toward the vision.

Getting Started

Welcome participants as they arrive. Have people form groups of three, with a mixture of ages in each group. When groups have formed, **SAY:** I want each of you to think of something you've always wanted to be or do and share it with others in your group. It can be anything at all, including something you already are. As the leader, model what you want by telling about something you've dreamed of being or doing. For example, you might have dreamed about taking a trip to Africa.

When everyone has shared within the small groups, **SAY:** Now suppose you were really going to follow that dream. What would you start doing now? What steps would you take? As the leader, give examples based on the dream you shared. If your dream is a trip to Africa, you might start saving money, reading travel books, and talking to people who have been there. If people are already pursuing their dream (or have already done it), have them describe the steps they have taken.

After people have shared in their groups, ask volunteers to tell the whole group about some of the ideas. Then ask:

• **How does enthusiasm for the dream give energy and motivation for actually working on it?**

What You'll Need

For the leader and group activities:
■ "Our Picture of the Future" newsprint from session 3
■ newsprint and easel
■ bold, nontoxic markers
■ masking tape

For each participant:
■ a copy of Work Sheet 18 (pp. 114-115), Work Sheet 19 (p. 116), Work Sheet 20 (p. 117), and Work Sheet 21 (p. 118)
■ a pen or pencil

• What barriers make it hard to plan for fulfilling that dream? For example, your dream might be to become a professional athlete, but that won't be accomplished if you're not good in sports. We're much more likely to pursue our dreams if they are consistent with our personality and gifts. We're also more likely to pursue them if they are not so lofty that they are overwhelming and seemingly impossible to reach.

• What could you do to keep yourself on track in pursuing your dream?

Post the "Our Picture of the Future" newsprint from session 3, and review what the group wrote. **THEN SAY: We created a picture of the future for youth ministry in our congregation. You might say it's one of our "dreams" or visions for youth ministry. It would be easy not to act on that dream for many of the same reasons that we don't always act on our personal dreams. But there are practical things we can start doing now that will help us move in the direction of that vision.**

Invite people to comment on similarities between how they work toward their own personal dreams and how the congregation might work toward this vision for youth ministry.

Turning a Vision Into Action

SAY: Last time we focused on one or two main ideas for strengthening our youth ministry. There are probably many other things we could do as well. But for now, we're going to focus on these priorities. This way we won't get overwhelmed, and we'll have a chance to practice building a vision-based plan. Later, we may decide to work toward strengthening some other areas of our youth program.

Remind people that the focus of your vision is the future of youth ministry in your congregation. Explain that Search Institute has identified six keys, or touchstones, for effective change in congregations. If your congregation consciously does these six things, it will be more likely to be successful in achieving its vision.

Distribute Work Sheet 18, "Touchstones for Effective Change" (pp. 114-115). Briefly discuss each of the six "FUTURE" touchstones. Then form three small groups. (If you have more than twelve people, form one group for each touchstone.) Assign each group two of the touchstones, and give each group several sheets of newsprint. For example, one group might take "Free People to Participate" and "Use Input of Thought-Leaders."

Have each group focus on its first touchstone and brainstorm about ways to address this touchstone in working toward your vision. For example, if your vision involves a new emphasis on youth leadership in the congregation, what values and traditions in the congregation can be built on in making that vision a reality? Use Work Sheet 18 to help guide the discussion.

Give each group about ten minutes to brainstorm on the first assigned touchstone while one group member records all the ideas on newsprint. Then have each group pick the two most important ideas from the brainstorm list. Have each group report its two ideas to the larger group, and record them on newsprint. Then do the same thing with the groups' second assigned touchstones.

Building Support for Your Vision

SAY: Sometimes when we plan, it's easy to think that nothing will really happen unless someone else does something. So we wait for other people or groups to make decisions or take action. Often we get discouraged because nothing seems to change. But there are things each of us can do personally to work toward this vision. In fact, it's probably best for us to start where we are with the things we can influence and then decide where to go next with our ideas. Search Institute has identified some important steps in building support for and involvement in a vision. This approach begins with an individual commitment and gradually expands to include others.

Distribute Work Sheet 19, "Widening Your Circle of Support" (p. 116). Briefly explain each circle, using the background information on Work Sheet 20 (p. 117), which you may also choose to distribute. Then ask people to do the following:

• **In the center circle, write one specific way you will personally commit to making our vision become a reality.** Give time for people to do this.

• **Who beyond this group do you trust to talk with and share the vision to get their support? In the next ring (labeled "Find Support from Like-Minded People"), write the names of one or two people you will contact.**

When people have finished, ask volunteers to share their commitments and contacts. (Don't insist that everyone share, just those who are comfortable.) As a group, brainstorm about how you might approach the next three circles of support.

Next Steps: Brainstorming

As a group, brainstorm some next steps that would move your congregation closer to the vision for your youth ministry, keeping in mind the strategies you developed (based on the "FUTURE" touchstones) and the circles of support. Encourage people to identify actions they personally can take that could contribute to the vision, not just the big ideas for someone else.

Use Work Sheet 21 to identify what needs to happen next, who is responsible for those action steps, and when those actions will be completed.

Closing: Thanks and Thanksgiving

Invite people to hold hands in a circle. **SAY:** **These four planning sessions represent an important chapter in the life of this congregation and its youth ministry. Each of you has given a gift of your time, your creativity, your commitment, and your vision to our work together. I really appreciate what each of you brings to this congregation and its youth.**

Then invite people each to share something they have been thankful for in the planning process. They might first thank others in the room and other people in the congregation, and then offer thanks to God for leadership, guidance, vision, and strength. If your congregation has a particular ritual or benediction, use it to conclude the session.

Work Sheet 18

Touchstones for Effective Change

Through extensive research on organizational change, Search Institute has identified six touchstones*—or reference points—to keep in mind as you work to plan and bring about change in your congregation's youth ministry. Coming back to these touchstones again and again throughout your planning process will help you create and carry out a meaningful, substantive vision for your youth ministry. Here are the six touchstones, along with brief descriptions and questions for planning.

Free people to participate.

People are much more likely to be involved in planning and change if they feel comfortable, valued, and inspired. They must be assured—and see evidence—that what they say and do will be respected and considered worthwhile. Dissenters need to be respected and listened to, and participation needs to be a positive, energizing experience.

- What things can we do to make people feel good about the changes we are proposing?
- How will we respect and listen to people who resist the proposed changes? How can we learn from them without letting them become roadblocks to essential changes?

Unite around needs.

People usually change to meet a perceived need. The gap between their goals or ideals and the current realities must be readily apparent. People's inner desire for change is more powerful than persuasion from leaders.

- How will we gather information that will make the need for change clear and compelling?
- What strengths of the congregation and youth ministry can be emphasized as we identify needs?

Tie in to mission and values.

Each congregation and youth ministry is unique, and plans for the future must build on the congregation's history, beliefs, and sense of purpose. Before introducing changes into a congregation, it's important to show how these innovations tie in to the congregation's mission and identity. New ideas that are compatible with cherished values and practices are more likely to be embraced.

- How do our new ideas tie in to or build on the congregation's history, theology, mission, and priorities?
- How can we show ways the proposed changes would help nurture spiritual growth in young people?

Use input of thought-leaders.

People are most influenced by "thought-leaders." They are people we trust and respect, people we feel comfortable with, and people with contagious enthusiasm. There are many thought-leaders, in both formal and

---

*Touchstone: A crystalline rock used to test the purity of gold or silver. If the metal is genuine, it leaves a streak when rubbed on the touchstone.

informal roles, who exert influence. Keeping them informed, seeking their opinions, and asking for their support will help promote an innovative atmosphere.

- Who in the congregation do people look up to? (Think of people in formal roles, such as a pastor, and informal roles, such as a well-liked senior citizen or young adult. Keep in mind people who are influential among youth.)
- How can we keep these people informed and involved in our plans? How can we nurture their support for our vision?

Rally broad support.

Ownership by people involved in change is crucial to its adoption. Although involving many people in creating an inspiring vision is difficult, it's also an enormously valuable and powerful experience. It's especially important to involve people who have a stake in the change or will be asked to implement it.

- Who are the important stakeholders and implementers in the congregation who need to be involved in shaping the vision for youth ministry?
- How will we keep many people in the congregation informed about and involved in the planning?

Engage in action.

Creating planned change requires discipline and a deep commitment to action. Four points are essential: (1) Be clear about your mission and how you will carry it out; (2) carefully plan start-ups, including some pilot efforts or "trial runs"; (3) do it, fix it, try it again; and (4) create structures to sustain the innovation long-term.

- Who in the congregation is good at planning and carrying out those plans? How can we involve these members in this process?
- What would be some ways to do low-risk trial runs to see how our plan works and to learn about how to be more effective?
- How can these changes be integrated into the congregation's structure so that they are sustained?

Work Sheet 19
Widening Your Circle of Support

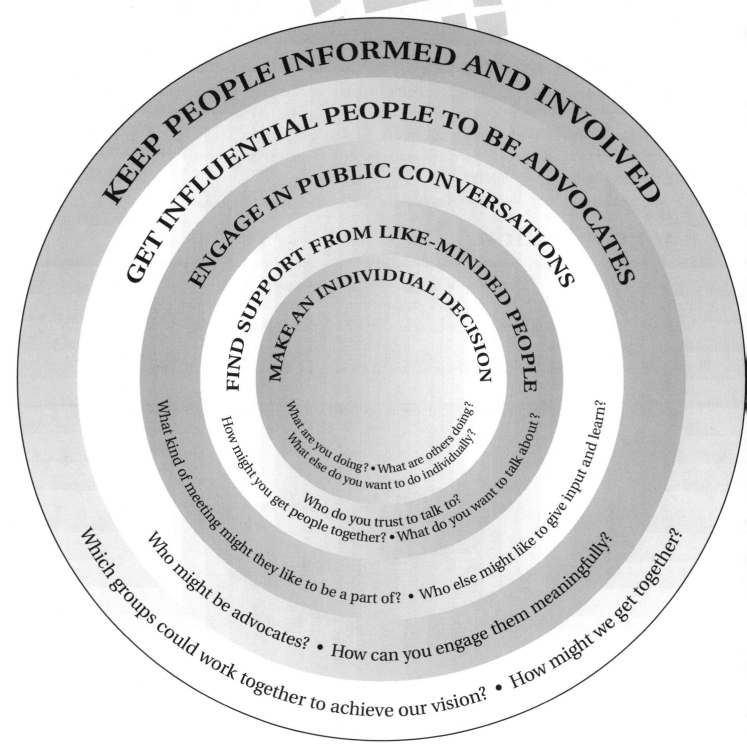

KEEP PEOPLE INFORMED AND INVOLVED

GET INFLUENTIAL PEOPLE TO BE ADVOCATES

ENGAGE IN PUBLIC CONVERSATIONS

FIND SUPPORT FROM LIKE-MINDED PEOPLE

MAKE AN INDIVIDUAL DECISION

What are you doing? • What are others doing?
What else do you want to do individually?

Who do you trust to talk to?

How might you get people together? • What do you want to talk about?

What kind of meeting might they like to be a part of? • Who else might like to give input and learn?

Who might be advocates? • How can you engage them meaningfully?

Which groups could work together to achieve our vision? • How might we get together?

Work Sheet 20

Background to Widening the Circle of Support

Search Institute has identified five steps in building support and involvement for a vision. This approach begins with an individual commitment and gradually expands to include others.

1. Make an individual decision.

Action begins when an individual decides to take action and then follows through.

• What are you already doing to bring this vision closer to a reality?

• What else might you personally do to make the vision come closer to a reality?

2. Find support from like-minded people.

Talk with trusted people who can help you learn more about the issues and possible solutions to challenges in the area you're working on.

• Who are some individuals you trust with whom you could talk about these ideas and from whom you could get feedback? How will you make it a priority to talk with them?

• How will you bring information from your conversations back to this group?

3. Engage in public conversations.

Instead of trying to "sell" your idea to the congregation's leaders, sponsor a "public conversation," in which interested people can talk together about the idea and give their input.

• What other individuals and groups might want to be involved in a public conversation?

• What kind of meeting would these people attend? When and how could you sponsor it?

4. Get influential people to be advocates.

A group of influential people who are committed to your vision can be critical to getting the congregation to invest in and support the vision.

• What people or groups might be willing to be advocates for your vision?

• How could you present your vision in a way that would motivate them to support it?

5. Keep people informed and involved.

Keep lots of people and groups in the congregation informed of what you are doing and how they can help.

• What opportunities do you have to communicate the vision to the congregation?

• What are simple ways other people can get involved in the vision?

Work Sheet 21
Our Action Plan

Priority Action

Write your priority area—from the "Our Picture of the Future" newsprint—in this space.

Actions Needed	Who's Responsible	By When?
1.		
2.		
3.		
4.		
5.		

If this group is meeting again to review progress, when will that be?

_____

If needed, how will this action plan be communicated to others in the congregation? Who needs to know about it? Who will communicate it?

_____

_____

Action Plan:
Putting the Pieces Together

The Congregations at Crossroads study identified critical needs to be addressed in congregations. On the one hand, this information could be disheartening. There is so much that needs to be done, there are so many areas that need attention. Yet the research actually has a positive focus. Rather than dealing only with all the problems, the study gives a practical, concrete framework for moving forward. It tells us what specific areas need to be addressed to begin turning the tide. This book highlights the dozens of ways congregations can strengthen their youth ministries to nurture the faith of young people. So where do you start? Here are some suggestions.

1. Bring People Together

Planning a youth ministry direction should not be the sole responsibility of the youth worker or even of those responsible for implementing the programs. Draw many different people into the discussion—young people, parents, the senior pastor, other youth ministry volunteers, and other members of the congregation. Share the information from the study and begin to build a shared understanding of and commitment to a youth ministry focused on nurturing faith.

2. Focus the Vision

Perhaps it's obvious, but it's important to clearly articulate the focus of youth ministry. There are many comprehensive methods for developing this shared understanding. For the purposes of this book, it's enough to highlight the need to be explicit in naming why we do what we do in youth ministry. Write your purpose in the center circle on Work Sheet 22 (p. 121).

3. Identify and Celebrate Current Efforts That Contribute to the Focus

One of the things we sometimes forget to do is identify and celebrate the strengths and resources that are already in place. Virtually every congregation has strengths to celebrate. These strengths become a strong foundation upon which to build. These strengths may be full-fledged programs, or they may be individuals with commitment and energy. Take time to remember and honor these strengths. Write them in the first ring outside the center circle on Work Sheet 22, and keep them in mind as you explore new directions.

4. Identify Other Priorities That Must Be Addressed

In addition, as you reviewed the checklists and ideas in this book, you likely identified some key areas that need to be addressed. Perhaps they involve getting more people connected to youth. Perhaps they focus on Bible study. Or perhaps they emphasize youth leadership. Your focus must fit your own congregation's context, history, and vision. Write these emphases in the second circle on Work Sheet 22.

5. Examine and Let Go of Programs That Are Not Essential

In the process of reflecting on your youth ministry, you may have discovered that some of the areas into which you currently put a lot of energy are no longer priorities. These areas are not contributing significantly to your congregation's central focus for ministry. In these cases, it may be time to let go of these efforts. Write these outside the circles on Work Sheet 22. Talk to the people involved to be sure that you fully understand what they are doing and its impact. (You may discover that the program is more essential than you first imagined!) Letting go of particular programs is not the same as "dumping" them. Take time to celebrate the impact and commitment the programs represent. Find ways to honor those who carried out the programs—and find other places where they can use their talents and gifts.

6. Connect Youth Ministry to the Whole Congregation's Ministries

Perhaps it's already clear or should be assumed, but too often congregations plan youth ministry in isolation from the larger community of faith. The result is a perpetuation of the separation of youth and youth ministry from the rest of the church. As you think about involving youth in service, for example, you don't have to think automatically of creating new programs or opportunities. Are there service and volunteer activities already happening for adults that would be appropriate for young people as well? Or what about an interactive Bible study for youth and adults together? Yes, there are particular challenges and barriers to overcome, but the benefits can far outweigh the challenges in the long term.

Only when youth ministry is reconnected to the larger mission and ministry of the church will people throughout the congregation begin to see their personal responsibility for and stake in nurturing the faith of young people. And only then will young people have the opportunity to be enriched through relationships with older members of the congregation. And only then will you discover all the rich resources that already exist in the congregation for nurturing the faith of youth.

7. Give It—and Yourself—Time

Sometimes we get so excited about the potential that we forget how long it can take to reach that potential in youth ministry. It may take several weeks just to get a committee together to talk about ideas. And some changes you might like to see involve getting many different people on board. So give yourself time. Celebrate the small ways that things improve. Years from now, you—or those who follow you—will look back and see how those little things set in motion important changes that have had an impact on many generations of youth who have been touched by your congregation's ministry.

Work Sheet 22
Focusing Your Youth Ministry

• What is the central focus of your youth ministry? What do you seek to accomplish? Write your response in the bull's-eye of the target.

• What are the current programs or emphases in your congregation that are essential to supporting this central focus? Write them in the first ring of the target. What can you do in the next two months to celebrate and strengthen these programs?

• What new programs or emphases do you see as being essential for strengthening your focus? Write them in the second ring. What can you do in the next two months to begin building toward those programs?

• What other programs do you offer for youth that are not essential to your central purpose? Write them in the space surrounding the target. What can you do in the next two months to either reshape these programs to address your focus or phase out these programs?

ACTION PLAN

Afterword: Change Takes Time

When you're watching young people face difficult issues, it's natural to want to jump in and find immediate solutions. You likely have sat on youth committees that think once-a-month pizza parties for youth after football games will solve complicated problems. You want to participate in more meaningful change and more effective solutions. Yet you know—and research confirms—that change takes time.

When significant change occurs, it's because of the thoughtful work of members and leaders in a community over a sustained period of time. Rarely does a group see significant change in the first year of work; it's more likely to be three or four years before you see results.

Why does change take so much time? A few reasons:

■ It takes time to gather good information on challenges, resources, and solutions.

■ It takes time to ask other people to share their concerns and ideas.

■ It takes time to develop a shared vision of the kind of congregation you want for the benefit of children and youth.

■ It takes time for you and everyone involved to change personal commitments so that you can maintain balance in your lives as you try to start something new.

■ It takes time for a congregation to adjust to new ways of doing things, even when the people involved are committed to the change. If some aren't committed, it takes even longer.

■ It takes time to act; it takes time to reflect on what is happening because of your actions; it takes time to change course as circumstances change.

But just because change takes time doesn't mean that nothing can happen soon. One of the most important decisions a group can make is to plan for some early successes so that you can demonstrate the value of working together and achieving a goal that couldn't have been achieved by one person alone. Whatever option you choose, it's important to remember that your efforts do matter and that each positive action for youth makes your congregation a better place.

Resource Publishers

Below are the addresses and phone numbers for the publishers of books and other materials listed in the "Resources to Use" sections throughout this book. Many of the resources are also available through local bookstores.

Abingdon Press
201 Eighth Ave. South
Box 801
Nashville, TN 37202
1-800-251-3320

Alban Institute
Suite 433 North
4550 Montgomery Ave.
Bethesda, MD 20814
1-800-486-1318

Augsburg Fortress Publishers
426 S. Fifth St.
Box 1209
Minneapolis, MN 55440
1-800-328-4648

Ave Maria
Campus of Notre Dame
Notre Dame, IN 46556
1-800-282-1865

Concordia Publishing House
3558 S. Jefferson Ave.
St. Louis, MO 63118
1-800-325-3040

Free Spirit Publishing
400 First Ave. North, Ste. 616
Minneapolis, MN 55401
1-800-735-7323

Group Publishing
1515 Cascade Avenue
Loveland, CO 80538
1-800-447-1070

InterVarsity Press
Box 1400
Downers Grove, IL 60515
1-800-843-7225

LCMS Department of Youth Ministry
1333 S. Kirkwood Rd.
St. Louis, MO 63122
(314) 965-9000 ex. 1162

Leadership Network
Box 9100
Tyler, TX 75711
1-800-765-5323

Religious Education Press
5316 Meadow Brook Dr.
Birmingham, AL 35243
1-800-937-8000

Search Institute
700 S. Third St., Ste. 210
Minneapolis, MN 55415
1-800-888-7828

St. Mary's Press
702 Terrace Heights
Winona, MN 55987
1-800-533-8095

Youth and Family Institute of Augsburg College
Campus Box #70
2211 Riverside Ave.
Minneapolis, MN 55454
1-877-239-2492

Youth Specialties
Order Center
Box 4406
Spartanburg, SC 29305
1-800-776-8008

Endnotes

1. See Eugene C. Roehlkepartain, *Building Assets in Congregations: A Practical Guide for Helping Youth Grow Up Healthy* (Minneapolis: Search Institute, 1998) as well as other resources on "developmental assets."

2. As part of this study, this mark of faith was added to the original Faith Maturity Scale, which included eight marks of faith and thirty-eight items.

3. "From Mass Evangelism to Relational Evangelism," Congregations (March/April 1996).

4. Kennon L. Callahan, *Twelve Keys to an Effective Church* (San Francisco: Harper & Row, 1983), 24-33.

5. John Killinger, "Reviving the Rites of Worship," Leadership (Fall 1989), 82-86.

6. Stephen P. West, "Making Worship Youth-Friendly," Circuit Rider (March 1995).

7. Eugene C. Roehlkepartain, *The Teaching Church: Moving Christian Education to Center Stage* (Nashville: Abingdon, 1993), 167-179.

8. "Why Youth Ministry Should Be Abolished," GROUP Magazine (July/August 1995).

9. Peter C. Scales et al., *The Attitudes and Needs of Religious Youth Workers: Perspectives From the Field* (Minneapolis: Search Institute, 1995), 10.

Group Publishing, Inc.
Attention: Product Development
P.O. Box 481
Loveland, CO 80539
Fax: (970) 679-4370

Evaluation for
Strategic Youth Ministry

Please help Group Publishing, Inc. continue to provide innovative and useful resources for ministry. Please take a moment to fill out this evaluation and mail or fax it to us. Thanks!

● ● ●

1. As a whole, this book has been (circle one)

not very helpful   very helpful

1   2   3   4   5   6   7   8   9   10

2. The best things about this book:

3. Ways this book could be improved:

4. Things I will change because of this book:

5. Other books I'd like to see Group publish in the future:

6. Would you be interested in field-testing future Group products and giving us your feedback? If so, please fill in the information below:

Name _____

Church Name _____

Denomination _____ Church Size _____

Church Address _____

City _____ State _____ ZIP _____

Church Phone _____

E-mail _____

Bible Study Series

Give Your Teenagers a Solid Faith Foundation That Lasts a Lifetime!

Here are the *essentials* of the Christian life—core values teenagers *must* believe to make good decisions now...and build an *unshakable* lifelong faith. Developed by youth workers like you...field-tested with *real* youth groups in *real* churches...here's the meat your kids *must* have to grow spiritually—presented in a fun, involving way!

Each 4-session **Core Belief Bible Study Series** book lets you easily...

● Lead deep, compelling, *relevant* discussions your kids won't want to miss...

● Involve teenagers in exploring life-changing truths...

● Help kids create healthy relationships with each other—and you!

Plus you'll make an *eternal difference* in the lives of your kids as you give them a solid faith foundation that stands firm on God's Word.

Here are the Core Belief Bible Study Series titles already available...

Senior High Studies

Why **Authority** Matters	0-7644-0892-5
Why **Being a Christian** Matters	0-7644-0883-6
Why **Creation** Matters	0-7644-0880-1
Why **Forgiveness** Matters	0-7644-0887-9
Why **God** Matters	0-7644-0874-7
Why **God's Justice** Matters	0-7644-0886-0
Why **Jesus Christ** Matters	0-7644-0875-5
Why **Love** Matters	0-7644-0889-5
Why **Our Families** Matter	0-7644-0894-1
Why **Personal Character** Matters	0-7644-0885-2
Why **Prayer** Matters	0-7644-0893-3
Why **Relationships** Matter	0-7644-0896-8
Why **Serving Others** Matters	0-7644-0895-X
Why **Spiritual Growth** Matters	0-7644-0884-4
Why **Suffering** Matters	0-7644-0879-8
Why **the Bible** Matters	0-7644-0882-8
Why **the Church** Matters	0-7644-0890-9
Why **the Holy Spirit** Matters	0-7644-0876-3
Why **the Last Days** Matter	0-7644-0888-7
Why **the Spiritual Realm** Matters	0-7644-0881-X
Why **Worship** Matters	0-7644-0891-7

Junior High/Middle School Studies

The Truth About **Authority**	0-7644-0868-2
The Truth About **Being a Christian**	0-7644-0859-3
The Truth About **Creation**	0-7644-0856-9
The Truth About **Developing Character**	0-7644-0861-5
The Truth About **God**	0-7644-0850-X
The Truth About **God's Justice**	0-7644-0862-3
The Truth About **Jesus Christ**	0-7644-0851-8
The Truth About **Love**	0-7644-0865-8
The Truth About **Our Families**	0-7644-0870-4
The Truth About **Prayer**	0-7644-0869-0
The Truth About **Relationships**	0-7644-0872-0
The Truth About **Serving Others**	0-7644-0871-2
The Truth About **Sin and Forgiveness**	0-7644-0863-1
The Truth About **Spiritual Growth**	0-7644-0860-7
The Truth About **Suffering**	0-7644-0855-0
The Truth About **the Bible**	0-7644-0858-5
The Truth About **the Church**	0-7644-0899-2
The Truth About **the Holy Spirit**	0-7644-0852-6
The Truth About **the Last Days**	0-7644-0864-X
The Truth About **the Spiritual Realm**	0-7644-0857-7
The Truth About **Worship**	0-7644-0867-4